W9-CNQ-503

Better Homes and Gardens®

Christmas At Home

BETTER HOMES AND GARDENS® BOOKS
Des Moines, Iowa

Better Homes and Gardens® Books
An imprint of Meredith Books

Better Homes and Gardens® *Christmas At Home*
Editors, Crafts: Sara Jane Treinen, Patricia Wilen
Editors, Food: Shelli McConnell, Mary Jo Plutt
Graphic Designer: Tom Wegner
Project Manager: Liz Anderson

Associate Art Director: Linda Ford Vermie
Food Stylists: Janet Herwig, Jennifer Peterson
Contributing Photo Stylist: Patty Konecny
Contributing Illustrator: Chris Neubauer
Contributing Editor: Deanna West
Publishing Systems Text Processor: Paula Forest

Meredith® Books
Editor in Chief: James D. Blume
Design Director: Matt Strelecki
Managing Editor: Gregory H. Kayko

Director, Sales & Marketing, Retail: Michael A. Peterson
Director, Special Markets: Rita McMullen
Director, Sales & Marketing, Home & Garden Center Channel: Ray Wolf
Director, Operations: Valerie Wiese

Vice President, General Manager: Jamie Martin

***Better Homes and Gardens®* Magazine**
Editor in Chief: Jean LemMon

Meredith Publishing Group
President, Publishing Group: Christopher M. Little
Vice President and Publishing Director: John P. Loughlin

Meredith Corporation
Chairman of the Board: Jack D. Rehm
President and Chief Executive Officer: William T. Kerr

Chairman of the Executive Committee: E.T. Meredith III

All of us at Better Homes and Gardens Books are dedicated to providing you with the information and ideas you need to enhance your home. We welcome your comments and suggestions about this book. Write to us at: Better Homes and Gardens Books, Editorial Department, RW206, 1716 Locust St., Des Moines, IA 503093023.

Our seal assures you that every recipe in *Christmas at Home* has been tested in the *Better Homes and Gardens®* Test Kitchen. This means that each recipe is practical and reliable, and meets our high standards of taste appeal. We guarantee your satisfaction with this book for as long as you own it.

Copyright © 1997 by Meredith Corporation, Des Moines, Iowa.
All rights reserved. Printed in the United States of America.
First Edition. Printing Number and Year: 5 4 3 2 1   01 00 99 98 97
Library of Congress Catalog Card Number: 91-68535
ISBN: 0-696-20768-0

*May these pages inspire you
to create beautiful gifts,
warm memories to cherish,
and a home blessed with the
fragrant and festive
trappings of a joyous
Christmas season.*

Contents

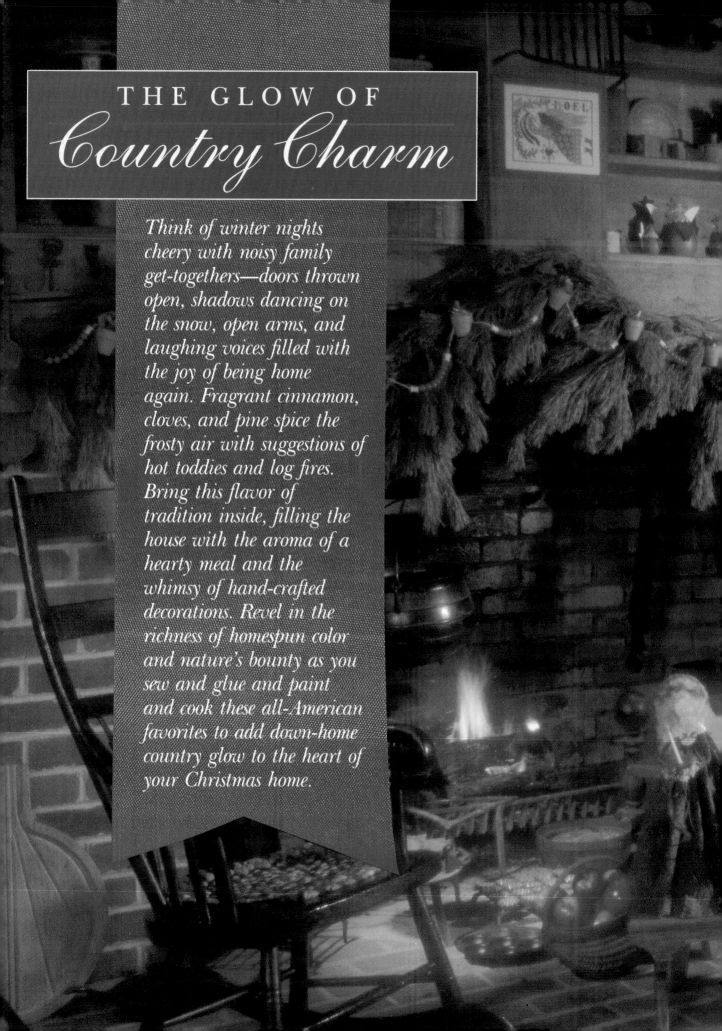

THE GLOW OF
Country Charm

Think of winter nights cheery with noisy family get-togethers—doors thrown open, shadows dancing on the snow, open arms, and laughing voices filled with the joy of being home again. Fragrant cinnamon, cloves, and pine spice the frosty air with suggestions of hot toddies and log fires. Bring this flavor of tradition inside, filling the house with the aroma of a hearty meal and the whimsy of hand-crafted decorations. Revel in the richness of homespun color and nature's bounty as you sew and glue and paint and cook these all-American favorites to add down-home country glow to the heart of your Christmas home.

Spool Tree Topper

Angel is approximately 9 inches tall.

MATERIALS

Thirteen ¾x1-inch wooden spools
Nine ½x⅝-inch wooden spools
Four ⁹⁄₁₆-inch-diameter wooden
    beads
One 1¾-inch-diameter wooden
    bead for head
Two ⅜-inch-diameter red beads
1¾ yards of jute twine
6x22-inch piece of muslin for dress
6-inch square of prequilted print
    fabric for heart-shaped wings
1-inch-square scraps of red and
    green print fabrics
14 inches of ¾-inch-wide star
    garland for halo
12 inches of narrow gold cord for
    spool garland
7 to 8 inches of crepe-wool hair
Bathroom tissue cardboard tube
Hot-glue gun
Black and red fine-tipped perma-
    nent markers for facial features
Cosmetic blush for cheeks

INSTRUCTIONS

Follow instructions for the spool tree
ornament, *opposite*, to make the tree
topper. Use two large spools for each
arm, three large spools for the trunk
of the body, and three large spools
for each leg.

Cut a 1-inch slit at the top edge of
the dress fabric 5 inches from each
end. Make dress in the same manner
as for the ornament. Add wings, hair,
and details as described.

String small spools and beads onto
the gold cord as desired. Wrap the
ends of the cord between the last
spool and the bead on each arm to
hold it in place. If desired, glue extra
stars from the halo onto the cord.

Glue cardboard tube vertically to
back of wings. Position angel on the
tree by slipping tube over the top-
most limb.

Spool Garland

MATERIALS

For one 10-foot-long garland
165 ¾x1-inch wooden spools
57 ⅜-inch-diameter red beads
3½ yards of jute twine

INSTRUCTIONS

Tie a knot in one end of the jute.
String a bead onto the jute, then
three spools and another bead. Continue adding spools and beads in this
manner. When all spools and beads
are strung, tie a knot in the untied
end of the jute to hold them in place.

Spool Tree Ornament

Finished ornament is 3½ inches tall.

MATERIALS

Seven ½x⅝-inch wooden spools
One ¾-inch-diameter wooden bead
    for the head
Four ⅜-inch-diameter wooden
    beads
1 yard of jute twine
2¼x10-inch piece of dress fabric
3-inch square of prequilted print
    fabric for heart-shaped wings
½-inch-square scraps of red and
    green print fabrics
6 inches *each* of ⅛-inch-wide ribbon
    and ⅛-inch-wide star garland
2½ inches of crepe-wool hair
8 inches of gold cording for hanger
One small eye screw; Hot-glue gun
Black and red fine-tipped perma-
    nent markers for facial features
Cosmetic blush for cheeks

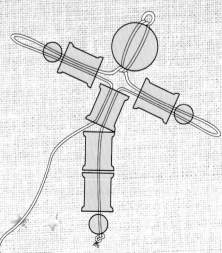

FIGURE 1

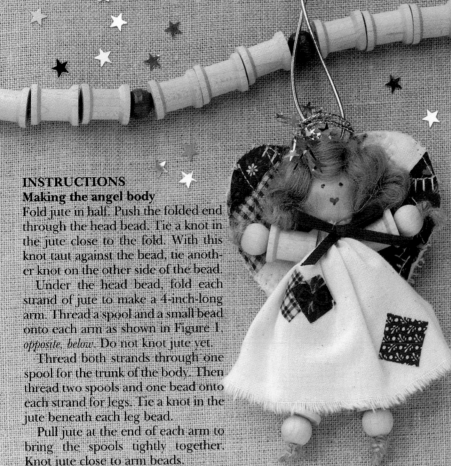

INSTRUCTIONS
Making the angel body
Fold jute in half. Push the folded end through the head bead. Tie a knot in the jute close to the fold. With this knot taut against the bead, tie another knot on the other side of the bead.

Under the head bead, fold each strand of jute to make a 4-inch-long arm. Thread a spool and a small bead onto each arm as shown in Figure 1, *opposite, below.* Do not knot jute yet.

Thread both strands through one spool for the trunk of the body. Then thread two spools and one bead onto each strand for legs. Tie a knot in the jute beneath each leg bead.

Pull jute at the end of each arm to bring the spools tightly together. Knot jute close to arm beads.

Trim excess jute at all knots.

Adding the dress and details
For armholes, cut a ¾-inch slit at the top edge of the dress fabric 2¼ inches from each end. Hand-sew a gathering stitch ¼ inch from the top edge of the fabric, stitching across the slits. Ravel or pink remaining raw edges.

Center the gathered dress on the doll with its arms sticking through the slits. Pull the gathering thread tight to fit the dress around the doll's neck; secure thread at back.

Using a little glue, screw the eye screw into the knot at the top of the head; let glue dry. Loop cording through the eye and tie the ends. Glue hair atop head, covering jute knot and screw. Glue star garland on the hair, wrapping it in a halo shape.

Tie a ribbon bow; glue it onto the dress at the front neckline. Cut a heart of prequilted fabric for wings; glue it onto angel's back. Glue tiny fabric patches on dress at random.

With the black marker, make two dots on the face for eyes. Use the red marker to draw a smile. Lightly rub blush on the angel's cheeks.

Spool Birdhouse

Birdhouse measures 5¾ inches high.

MATERIALS
Scraps of ¼-inch-thick pine
One ¼-inch-diameter dowel
7 1½x⅝-inch wooden spools
One *each* ¾x1-inch wooden spool
  and 1x1¼-inch wooden spool
Four ice-cream sticks
½-inch wire brads; sandpaper
Wood glue or hot-glue gun
Acrylic paints in white, dark red,
  and dark green; antiquing stain
Clear satin spray finish
Small handsaw; razor knife
1-inch drill bit and drill

INSTRUCTIONS
Cut two 3½x5-inch wood pieces for the house front and back. On both pieces, mark the center top on one short side. Then, on both pieces, mark 3 inches from the bottom on each long side. Trim each piece, cutting a 50-degree angle from the center top to the mark at each side to form the pitch of the roof.

Drill a 1-inch-diameter hole in the front piece, centering it 1½ inches from the bottom of the board.

Cut two 3x4½-inch side pieces. Cut a 50-degree angle on one long edge (top) of each piece. Glue and nail sides to front and back.

Glue and nail a 4x5¾-inch wood piece to the bottom, positioning it flush with the back and sides of the house but extending it 1¼ inches in front for a porch. For the porch step, center, glue, and nail a 1x4-inch piece atop the floor.

Cut two 4x6-inch roof pieces; cut a 50-degree angle in one long edge of each piece. Matching angled edges, glue and nail roof pieces in place, extending roof over the front porch.

Cut two lengths of dowel to fit between the roof and the porch corners; glue and nail in place.

Referring to the photo, *above,* paint roof, porch, and house; let dry. Sand to achieve a weathered look. Apply stain to porch and house only.

Cut ice-cream sticks to fit under the roof in front; cut the ¾x1-inch spool in half lengthwise for shutters. Paint, stain, and glue pieces in place.

Cut bottom of the large spool at a 50-degree angle; glue to roof for a chimney. Cut remaining spools in half lengthwise. Glue nine spools along the roof peak and remaining spools onto the roof sides; trim as necessary to fit around chimney. Let glue dry. Paint roof. When dry, sand lightly; apply stain. Spray completed birdhouse with clear spray finish.

Reindeer Angel

The reindeer measures approximately 12 inches tall.

MATERIALS

¼ yard *each* of muslin for the body and plaid fabric for the dress
26-inch square of ivory-colored netting for wings
1 yard of ¹⁄₁₆-inch-wide satin ribbon
Scraps of ivory-colored knit fabric for the socks and jute for the hair
One chenille stem or pipe cleaner
Brown fabric paint; powdered blush
Clean sand or other heavy filling
Polyester fiberfill
Fine-tipped fabric markers in black, red, and green
Black and ivory carpet threads
Small beans or plastic pellets for the feed bag
One small jingle bell
Tracing paper, pencil, and ruler

INSTRUCTIONS

Cutting the fabrics

Trace the body, head, ear, and leg patterns, *opposite*. Cut out a paper template for each pattern; trace the outline of each shape on the muslin.

Cut two *each* of the body and head patterns and four *each* of the ear and leg patterns. From the remaining muslin, cut one 2⅛x9-inch strip for the arms, one 1x5⅛-inch strip for the antlers, and two 3x4½-inch pieces for the feed bag.

For the dress, cut two 7x11½-inch pieces of plaid fabric.

Assembling the reindeer body

Note: Use a ¼-inch-wide seam allowance throughout.

ARMS: Fold the arm strip in half lengthwise with right sides together. Machine-stitch along the long edge, leaving both ends open. Turn the strip right side out.

Find the center of the strip and mark it with a straight pin. Insert a tiny amount of filling on either side of the pin. Tie a knot over the pin to form the hands, leaving the pin in place to be sure the knot is centered.

Remove the pin and insert a little filling into the arms on both sides of the knot. Do not fill the arms tightly.

BODY: On one body piece, align the raw edges of the arms and the body at the X's indicated on the body pattern; baste the arms in place.

With right sides together and the arms sandwiched between them, sew the two body pieces together. Leave the neck edge open for turning.

Pull the arms out first to turn the body right side out. Pour sand into the body piece, filling approximately 2½ inches from the bottom. Stuff the remaining body cavity with filling. Hand-sew the neck opening closed.

LEGS: Sew two leg pieces together, leaving the top edge open; turn the leg right side out.

Fill the foot with approximately 2 inches of sand. Tie a knot in the leg 3 inches from the bottom of the foot. Do not add any additional filling. Turn in a ¼-inch-wide hem at the top of the leg; top-stitch close to the edge, sewing through all layers.

Prepare second leg in the same manner. Paint the foot of each leg with brown fabric paint; let dry.

Cut a 1½x2¾-inch strip of knit fabric for each sock. With right sides together, stitch the short ends of each strip together. Fold each sock in half lengthwise, right sides out, bringing the raw edges together and enclosing the stitched seam allowance.

Hot-glue the raw edges of each sock strip to the leg at the top of the brown shoe, matching center back seams. Let the glue dry, then fold the top of the strip down to cover the raw edges. For shoelaces, use approximately 8 inches of ivory-colored carpet thread to stitch a large X across the center front seam of each foot; tie the ends of the thread in a bow just under the sock cuff.

Glue or hand-sew the legs to the bottom of the body, just behind the bottom seam.

HEAD: Lay one head piece over the head pattern, *opposite*. Use a dark red marker to draw the reindeer's smile and heart-shaped nose. Use a black marker for the eyes and lightly-drawn freckles. Apply blush for cheeks.

Cut a 1-inch-long horizontal slit in the other head piece, cutting approximately ½ inch above and parallel to the chin line. With right sides facing, join the two pieces, sewing around the entire edge of the head. Turn the head right side out through the slit in the back piece. Stuff the head tightly, then hand-sew the slit closed.

Sew or glue the head securely to the body, aligning the slit at the back with the top of the neck.

ANTLERS: Fold the antlers strip in half lengthwise. Stitch along all the edges, leaving a 1-inch opening in the center of the long edge. Turn the strip right side out.

Cut a chenille stem or pipe cleaner approximately ½ inch longer than the finished antler strip. Turn under ¼ inch on each end so the sharp ends won't poke through the fabric. Push the stem into the muslin strip; whipstitch the opening closed.

Hand-sew the center of the antlers strip to the top of the head; shape antlers as desired. Stitch a bell onto one antler.

EARS: Stitch two ear pieces together, leaving the bottom edge open. Repeat for second ear. Turn both ears right side out. Apply blush to the center of each ear.

Pinch the bottom edges of each ear together, with the blush to the inside. Baste the bottom edges together to hold them in place. Glue the pinched ends to the head just in front of the antlers.

Glue a 1¼-inch-long piece of jute twine between the ears; let glue dry. Untwist the twine and separate the strands to make the reindeer's mane. Glue a small bow of ribbon between the mane and the antlers.

Making the dress and wings
Turn under a 1¼-inch-wide neckline hem on one long edge of each dress piece. Top-stitch each hem 1 inch from the folded edge, then stitch again ¾ inch from the fold to form a casement for the ribbon.

Position the two rectangles with right sides together, aligning the hem stitching. Pin the two layers together at the sides, inserting a pin 3¼ inches from the bottom (unhemmed) edge.

With right sides together, stitch both side seams, sewing from the bottom edge to the pin. Back-stitch at the end of each seam; remove the pin. Press seam allowances open.

Top-stitch a ¼-inch-wide hem on the bottom edge of the dress.

Cut the remaining ribbon in half; thread a piece of ribbon through each dress casement. Put the dress on the reindeer; position the arms over the dress front. Pull the ribbons tight, gathering the dress around the deer's neck; tie the ribbons in a bow at both sides.

Fold the netting in thirds, bringing the raw ends into the center. Keep folding the netting until you have a strip approximately 3x26 inches. Tie the strip into a fluffy bow; glue or sew the bow in place on the angel's back.

Making the feed sack
Sew the two feed sack pieces together along both long edges and one short edge, leaving the other end open. Turn the bag right side out.

Ravel the fabric on the open edge to make approximately ¼ inch of fringe. Use black carpet thread to sew a loose basting stitch around the bag approximately 1¼ inches from the open end. Leave enough thread at the ends to tie a bow.

Use markers to embellish the bag with the words "Reindeer Feed" and decorative drawings as desired.

Fill the bag with beans, plastic pellets, or polyester fiberfill up to the gathering stitch. Gather the thread slightly and tie a bow. Turn down the edge of the bag. Glue beans or brown plastic pellets onto the top of the bag to represent reindeer feed.

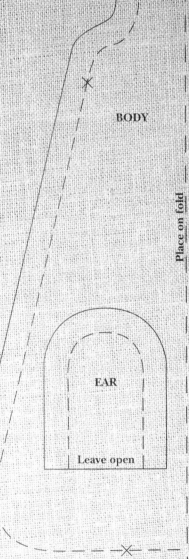

Stately Angel Doll

Doll is approximately 18 inches high.

MATERIALS

⅝ yard of cotton dress fabric
6-inch-diameter circle of muslin
4½-inch-diameter circle of gold
    lamé fabric for halo
1 yard *each* of ⅛-inch-wide ribbon
    in two coordinating colors
Lace-edged handkerchief or napkin
Fabric draping/stiffening solution
2-inch-long plastic foam egg for
    head; 5-inch-long wood or plastic
    pick to support head
Packaged curly doll hair
Assorted lace, tiny dried flowers,
    star-shaped confetti, and other
    trims as desired; small candle
Cap from a large toothpaste tube
Newspaper; cardboard scraps
28-gauge wire; tape
Hot-glue gun; white crafts glue

INSTRUCTIONS
Making the doll's body
Loosely roll up a 27-inch square of newspaper to make a tube. Bend the tube in half. Referring to Figure 1, *below*, wrap a wire around all layers 1½ inches below the fold, leaving approximately 1 inch of space between the two halves of the tube. Wrap a second piece of wire approximately 1½ inches below the first wire.

Roll up a 22-inch square of newspaper in the same manner, and bend it in half. Insert this tube into the space between the two wires as illustrated. Wrap wire around both rolls of paper to secure the body.

Roll a 22-inch newspaper square as tightly as possible; use tape to keep the tube tightly rolled. Thread this narrow tube through the body form above the first wire; trim it to 7 inches on each side of the shoulder.

Mount the plastic egg on one end of the pick, using glue to keep it in place. Position the egg atop the form, slipping the pick through the wires. Add tape to secure the pick.

Put the form in a drinking glass to hold it upright as you work.

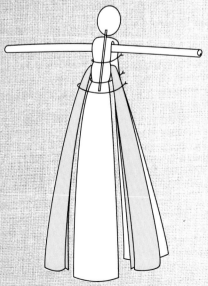

FIGURE 1

Sew two rows of basting around the muslin circle, ¼ inch from the edge. Center the muslin over the egg, then gather the fabric tight around the bottom. Adjust gathers at the back of the head; secure threads.

Making the doll's dress
Trim the selvages from the dress fabric. Cut or tear six ⅜x42-inch strips for the arms. Saturate the strips in a mixture of equal parts water and draping solution.

Starting at the end of the arm tube, wind wet strips tightly around one arm and then the other. Wrap strips around the shoulders and body in the same manner down to the first wire.

Cut a 13x42-inch rectangle for the skirt. Using matching thread, sew two rows of basting along one long side, ¼ inch from the edge. Top-stitch a ¼-inch-wide hem on the other three edges. Gather the skirt to fit the doll's waist, but do not secure it yet.

Saturate the skirt in the draping solution. Wrap the wet, gathered fabric around the doll's waist; hold it in place with a wrapping of wire to dry.

While the arms are still wet, bend them into position as desired. Use remaining liquid to remoisten the fabric if necessary. Wire or prop the arms in place until dry.

Drip draping solution onto the head until the muslin is wet. Smooth the fabric in front, adjusting gathers toward the back. Let the figure dry completely before continuing.

Cut a corner of an embroidered handkerchief to make a triangular collar piece; glue it in place around the neck. Glue ribbon or lace over the raw edge at the neck. Add a ribbon bow and other trim as desired.

Finishing details
Using hot glue, glue toothpaste cap to center back of head. Follow manufacturer's directions to put hair on head, parting the hair around the toothpaste cap and separating hair strands for a frizzy look.

Using crafts glue, cover a 3½-inch-diameter cardboard circle with lamé. Position the halo and glue it in place atop the toothpaste cap. Arrange hair to conceal the cap.

Glue dried flowers to the center of a 12-inch-long piece of ribbon, leaving approximately 2¾ inches bare at each end. Let glue dry. Place flower garland on hair and tie ribbon in back; trim excess ribbon.

For the doll's candle holder, cover a 2-inch-diameter cardboard circle with lamé. Glue dried flowers and stars around the edge and the candle in the center. Glue the candle holder atop the ends of the doll's arms.

Use the remaining ribbon to make a double bow with long streamers; glue bow in place at center front of candle holder.

Flowerpot Ornament

MATERIALS
2-inch-diameter terra-cotta pot
1-inch-diameter plastic foam ball
Assorted miniature ornaments
Spanish moss; cinnamon stick
Assorted candies, dried flowers,
  berries, miniature pinecones,
  potpourri, and other naturals
2 inches of heavy-gauge wire
White crafts glue; hot-glue gun

INSTRUCTIONS
Cover the foam ball with white glue; push ball into pot. Cover the top of the ball with Spanish moss; let glue dry. Hot-glue selected naturals and ornaments atop the moss as desired.

At the back of the decorated pot, push a 2-inch piece of cinnamon stick into the foam ball. Spread glue on the bottom half of the wire and push it into the foam, hiding it behind the cinnamon stick. Bend a loop in the top of the wire for hanging.

Flowerpot Garland

Instructions are for a garland approximately 10 feet long.

MATERIALS
5 yards (or desired length) of
  lightweight jute twine
14 Flowerpot Ornaments (see
  instructions, *right* and *above*)
144 ¾-inch-diameter red beads
Thirty ½x⅝-inch wooden spools
Hot-glue gun

INSTRUCTIONS
Make a knot in one end of the jute. String one spool onto the jute, then add 8 or 9 beads and another spool, pushing them down to the knot.

Next to the strung spool, glue the jute around the lip of one flowerpot; let glue dry. Continue adding beads, spools, and pots in this manner.

Arrange the flowerpot garland on a garland of pine boughs or drape the string around your tree, using the hanging wires to secure it.

Painted Wooden Angels

MATERIALS
For one set of three angels

One *each* of 2½-, 4-, and 5½-inch
  tall wooden eggs (available from
  Unfinished Business, Box 246,
  Dept. BHG, Wingate, NC 28174)
Scraps or one 12x16-inch piece of
  ⅛- or ¼-inch-thick plywood
Spanish moss
Six ½- to ¾-inch-long nails
Acrylic paints in the following
  colors: flesh, dark green, gold,
  dark red, black, and ivory
1-inch foam brushes
Small paintbrush for details
Paint thinner; matte acrylic spray
Antiquing medium; paper towels
Sandpaper
Hot-glue gun; band saw
Tracing and carbon papers

INSTRUCTIONS
Separately trace the three half-wing
and the star patterns, *left*, onto tracing paper; flip the paper to trace the
opposite side of each wing, joining
the two parts on the dotted line of the
pattern. Using carbon paper, trace
the patterns onto the plywood; cut
out the shapes. Sand the rough edges
until smooth. Keep pieces together
for each size of angel.

Cut off the large rounded bottom
of each egg; remove just enough to
create a flat surface so the egg will sit
upright. Using a foam brush, apply
flesh-colored paint to the top third of
each egg; let dry. Paint the bottom
part of each egg dark green. Paint the
stars gold, the wings ivory, and the
hearts dark red. When the paint is
completely dry, lightly sand the stars,
wings, and hearts.

Mix a small amount of antiquing
medium with paint thinner to obtain
a nice consistency for brush strokes.
Using a foam brush, spread the antiquing mixture on all pieces. Let the
antiquing medium set for approximately five minutes, then wipe off the
excess. Wait approximately 30 minutes before proceeding.

Use the detail brush to make two
little black dots on each angel's face
for eyes. Use a relatively dry brush to
dab light spots of dark red paint for
cheeks, then carefully paint tiny red
smiles. Paint a necklace of ivory dots
around the line where the flesh and
dark green colors meet.

Nail a heart to the front of each egg
just below the necklace; nail wings to
backs. Hot-glue a little Spanish moss
to the top of each egg for hair; glue
stars atop the moss. Let glue dry.

Spray the angels with matte acrylic
spray; let dry for approximately five
minutes before handling.

Appliquéd Tree Skirt and Stockings

Tree skirt is 56 inches in diameter.
Stockings measure 15 inches long.

MATERIALS

2¼ yards of 60-inch-wide plaid wool flannel (makes one skirt and two stockings; buy ¾ yard for an additional pair of stockings)
¼ yard *each* of three solid fabrics for appliqués; cookie cutters
Newspaper and graph paper
Assorted buttons and bells
Lightweight yarn or embroidery floss (optional)

INSTRUCTIONS

For the tree skirt

Cut a 56-inch square of newspaper. Refer to the drawings, *bottom, far right,* to fold the paper. Begin by folding it in half diagonally (A). Bring the triangle corners together, making a new triangle (B); fold a third time to form an even smaller triangle (C). Trim the triangle corners as illustrated (D).

Unfold the paper to check the eight-petaled shape; trim pattern to improve shape as desired.

Fold a 56-inch square of plaid fabric in the same manner. Using the paper pattern, cut the petal shape. To make an opening, cut on the fold between two petals. By machine or by hand, overcast all edges.

Using cookie cutters for patterns, cut appliqués from solid fabrics. Position shapes randomly. Appliqué by hand with a buttonhole stitch or with a machine satin stitch. Add buttons, embroidery, and trim as desired.

For the stockings

Cut a 15x30-inch rectangle of plaid fabric for each stocking. With wrong sides together, fold the rectangle in half to make a 15-inch square.

On graph paper, enlarge stocking pattern, *right.* Lay paper pattern atop folded fabric, placing it on the bias of the fabric. Cut through both layers, cutting front and back of stocking. Appliqué front as desired.

Match front and back with wrong sides together. Machine-stitch about ⅜ inch from the edge to sew the two pieces together. Leave the top edge open. Finish the raw edges with a

loose overcast stitch by machine (a serger is ideal) or work small buttonhole stitches by hand.

Cut a 5x15-inch straight-grained plaid strip for the cuff. Run a narrow machine satin stitch about 1 inch from one long edge. Pull out horizontal threads to create fringe. Appliqué name or initials in center of strip.

Sew the short ends of the strip together. Slip cuff inside stocking, with

right side of cuff against the wrong side of the stocking. Position cuff so the appliqué will be properly placed when turned to the right side. Align raw edges and sew cuff to stocking around the top edge. Turn cuff over seam allowance to the right side.

For the hanger, fold a 2½x8-inch plaid strip in half lengthwise. Sew the long edges together, using a ¼-inch-wide seam allowance. Turn right side out. Tack ends of strip to top inside corner of stocking.

Cut a 2¾x30-inch strip for the bow, tapering both ends. Overcast the edges. Bring the ends of the strip together, with wrong sides facing;
continued

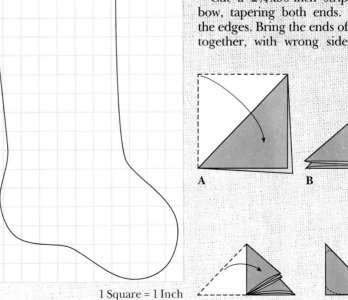

1 Square = 1 Inch

machine-stitch through both layers approximately 8 inches from the fold.

Flatten the fabric, with the seam at the center back. Use a 14-inch length of coordinating thread to hand-sew a gathering stitch through the center, sewing through both layers. Pull the thread to gather the fabric into a bow shape. Use the excess thread to tack the bow to the stocking's top corner.

Add buttons, bells, and other trim as desired.

Cross-Stitched Angel

Finished stitchery measures 6x8½ inches. Stitch count is 118 wide and 84 high.

MATERIALS
One 13x15-inch piece of 14-count oatmeal-colored Aida cloth
Two skeins of DMC embroidery floss in medium malachite (562), garnet (815), and medium old gold (729); one skein of each additional floss listed on key
Tapestry needle; embroidery hoop

INSTRUCTIONS
Referring to the chart, *opposite*, use three strands of floss and work cross-stitches over one square of the even-weave fabric. Center the design on the fabric. When cross-stitching is complete, work backstitches with one strand of floss. Frame as desired.

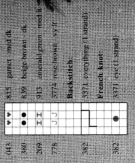

Anchor	DMC	
043	815	garnet - med dk
880	839	beige-brown - dk
209	913	emerald green - med lt
778	3774	rose-brown - vy lt
Backstitch		
382	3371	everything (1 strand)
French knot:		
382	3371	eye (1 strand)

Fabrics and finished design sizes:
11 Aida, 7-5/8"h x 10-3/4"w
14 Aida, 6"h x 8-1/2"w
18 Aida, 4-3/4"h x 6-5/8"w
22 Hardanger, 3-7/8"h x 5-3/8"w

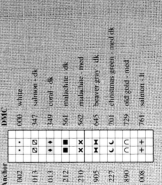

COLOR KEY

Anchor	DMC	
002	000	white
013	347	salmon - dk
013	349	coral - dk
212	561	malachite - dk
210	562	malachite - med
905	645	beaver gray - dk
227	701	christmas green - med dk
890	729	old gold - med
1008	761	salmon - lt

CROSS-STITCHED ANGEL

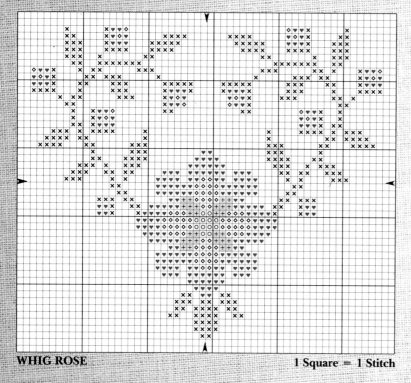

WHIG ROSE

1 Square = 1 Stitch

Tin Heart Ornament

Finished stitchery is approximately 2⅞x3⅛ inches. Stitch count is 51 wide and 55 high.

MATERIALS

Heart-shaped tin tart pan with
  scalloped edging approximately
  3¼ inches wide (Product No.
  021634, available from Cross
  Creek, telephone 800-678-2694)
6-inch square of 18-count Aida
  cloth
One skein of embroidery floss in
  each color listed on color key
Tapestry needle; embroidery hoop
9 inches of ¹⁄₁₆-inch-wide ribbon
4-inch square *each* of cardboard and
  polyester fleece or batting
White crafts glue; hot-glue gun
Tracing paper and pencil

INSTRUCTIONS

Following the chart for the Whig
Rose, *left;* Rose of Sharon, *opposite,
top;* or Berry Tree, *opposite, bottom,*

COLOR KEY

Anchor		DMC	
891	○ ○	676	old gold - lt
901	# #	680	old gold - dk
229	× ×	700	christmas green - dk
044	♥ ♥	816	garnet - med
382	■ ■	3371	black brown
035	◇ ◇	3705	strawberry - dk
028	+ +	3706	strawberry - med

Backstitch:

382		3371	birds' legs & beaks (2 strands)
229		700	stems (2 strands)

French knot:

382	●	3371	birds' eyes, berries (2 strands)

Fabrics and finished design sizes:

11 Aida, 5"h x 5"w
14 Aida, 4"h x 3-7/8"w
18 Aida, 3-1/8"h x 3"w
22 Hardanger, 2-1/2"h x 2-1/2"w

stitch the design of your choice. Center the motif on the Aida; use two strands of floss for cross-stitches and backstitches.

Holding the tracing paper over the tin heart, run a fingernail over the paper along the interior edge of the scalloped rim. Cut a heart-shaped paper pattern along the impression.

Use the pattern to mark and cut a heart of fleece and one of cardboard. Glue these together. Center the pattern on the wrong side of the stitched design. Trim fabric 1 inch *larger* than the pattern.

Center the stitchery atop the fleece heart. Pull the fabric edges over the fleece to the back of the cardboard; glue fabric edges in place. Hot-glue the covered heart in the center of the tart pan.

Fold ribbon in half. Insert the fold through the hole in the tin heart from the front; pull ribbon ends through the loop. Tie ends together in a knot.

ROSE OF SHARON   1 Square = 1 Stitch

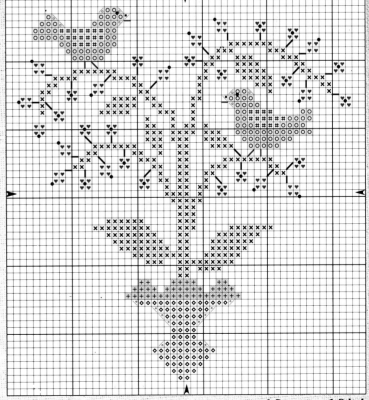

BERRY TREE   1 Square = 1 Stitch

COUNTRY
Christmas Eve Dinner

*Gathering for a homespun
dinner, singing around a
crackling fire, and sharing
treasured memories keeps the
eve of Christmas.*

Country Christmas Eve Dinner

Herbed Parmesan Bread
Pesto Spread
Roasted Red Pepper Spread
Country Pork Platter
Greens with Creamy Cucumber Dressing
Apple-Berry Ginger Pie

Timetable

Up to 3 months ahead
Prepare Herbed Parmesan Bread. Freeze.

2 days ahead
Prepare cabbage mixture for Country Pork Platter.
Cover and refrigerate.

1 day ahead
Wash and tear greens for salad. Place in plastic bag and refrigerate.
Prepare Roasted Red Pepper Spread and Pesto Spread.
Cover and refrigerate.

Several hours ahead
Prepare Creamy Cucumber Dressing for salad.
Cover and refrigerate.
Prepare and bake Apple-Berry Ginger Pie.

1 hour ahead
Let the Herbed Parmesan Bread stand at room temperature.

Herbed Parmesan Bread

5¼ to 5¾ cups all-purpose flour
2 packages active dry yeast
1 teaspoon salt
¼ teaspoon garlic powder
2 cups warm water (120° to 130°)
 Cornmeal
1 cup grated Parmesan cheese
2 teaspoons fines herbes, crushed
1 slightly beaten egg white
1 tablespoon water

In a large mixing bowl stir together *2 cups* of the flour, the yeast, salt, and garlic powder. Add the warm water. Beat with an electric mixer on low to medium speed for 30 seconds, scraping the sides of the bowl constantly. Then beat on high speed for 3 minutes. Using a wooden spoon, stir in as much of the remaining flour as you can.

Turn the dough out onto a lightly floured surface. Knead in enough of the remaining flour to make a stiff dough that is smooth and elastic (8 to 10 minutes total). Shape dough into a ball. Place the dough in a lightly greased bowl, turning once to grease the surface. Cover and let rise in a warm place till double in size (1 to 1½ hours).

Punch dough down. Turn out onto a lightly floured surface. Divide dough in half. Cover and let dough rest for 10 minutes. Lightly grease a large baking sheet. Sprinkle with cornmeal.

On a lightly floured surface, roll *each* portion of dough into a 15x12-inch rectangle. In a small mixing bowl stir together the Parmesan cheese and fines herbes. Sprinkle ½ cup of the cheese mixture over *each* dough rectangle to within 1 inch of the edges. Roll up each rectangle, jelly-roll style, starting from one of the long sides. Moisten edges and pinch seams to seal well. Taper ends.

Place the loaves seam sides down on the prepared baking sheet. Cover the loaves with a damp cloth and let them rise till *nearly* double (about 45 minutes).

Stir together the egg white and the 1 tablespoon water. Brush some of the egg white mixture over each loaf. Using a very sharp knife, make 5 or 6 diagonal cuts, about ¼ inch deep, across the tops of the loaves. Bake in a 375° oven for 40 to 45 minutes* or till loaves sound hollow when tapped with the tip of your finger (if necessary, cover loaves loosely with foil the last 15 minutes of baking to prevent overbrowning). Remove loaves from baking sheet and cool on a wire rack. Makes 2 loaves.

* For a crispier crust, after 20 minutes of baking, brush loaves again with the egg white mixture.

To freeze: Cool loaves completely, then wrap tightly in *heavy* foil or place in freezer bags or containers. Seal, label, and freeze for up to 3 months. Thaw the wrapped loaves at room temperature for 1 hour.

Pesto Spread

⅓ **cup purchased pesto**
½ **of an 8-ounce container soft-style cream cheese**

In a small mixing bowl stir together the pesto and cream cheese till well combined. Transfer the pesto mixture to a small serving bowl. Cover and refrigerate for at least 1 hour. Serve with sliced Herbed Parmesan Bread. Makes about ¾ cup.

Roasted Red Pepper Spread

¼ **cup chopped onion**
1 **clove garlic, minced**
1 **tablespoon olive oil** *or* **cooking oil**
1 **7-ounce jar roasted red peppers, drained**
¼ **teaspoon salt**
¼ **teaspoon dried thyme, crushed**
2 **tablespoons snipped parsley**

In a small saucepan cook the onion and garlic in olive oil or cooking oil till onion is tender but not brown. Cool slightly.

In a blender container or food processor bowl combine the onion-garlic mixture, roasted red peppers, salt, and thyme. Cover and blend or process with on-off turns till finely chopped

Transfer the pepper mixture to a small serving bowl. Stir in parsley. Cover and refrigerate for at least 1 hour. Serve with sliced Herbed Parmesan Bread. Makes ¾ cup.

Country Pork Platter

2 **slices thick-cut bacon, cut into 1-inch pieces**
1 **large onion, chopped (1 cup)**
2 **medium carrots, sliced (1 cup)**
2 **cloves garlic, minced**
½ **cup dry white wine**
2 **tablespoons brown sugar**
1 **tablespoon vinegar**
½ **teaspoon salt**
¼ **teaspoon pepper**
6 **cups shredded cabbage**
2 **red** *and/or* **green apples, cored and cubed**
10 **juniper berries (optional)**
12 **ounces fully cooked smoked bratwursts, knockwursts, frankfurters,** *and/or* **smoked sausage links, cut in half**
6 **fully cooked smoked boneless pork chops, cut ½ inch thick (about 2 pounds)**
1½ **pounds whole tiny new potatoes, boiled**
1 **tablespoon snipped parsley**

In a 4-quart Dutch oven cook the bacon till crisp. Using a slotted spoon, remove the bacon. Add the onion, carrots, and garlic to the Dutch oven. Cook and stir for 5 minutes.

Add the wine, brown sugar, vinegar, salt, and pepper to the cooked vegetable mixture. Stir in the cooked bacon, cabbage, apples, and, if desired, juniper berries. Bring mixture to boiling; reduce heat. Cover and simmer for 30 minutes. Transfer cabbage mixture to a large bowl. Cool slightly; cover and refrigerate for up to 2 days.

Before serving, transfer cabbage mixture to the Dutch oven. Nestle sausage pieces and pork chops into mixture. Heat to boiling; reduce heat. Cover and simmer about 30 minutes or till chops are heated through. Transfer to a large platter. Toss the hot boiled potatoes with the parsley. Transfer potatoes to a serving bowl. Serve with the meat and cabbage mixture. Makes 6 servings.

Greens with Creamy Cucumber Dressing

- 1 medium cucumber
- ½ cup dairy sour cream
- 2 green onions, sliced
- 2 tablespoons white wine tarragon vinegar *or* white wine vinegar
- 1 tablespoon salad oil
- ⅛ teaspoon dry mustard
- ⅛ teaspoon garlic powder
- 8 cups torn mixed greens

Cut the cucumber lengthwise in half. Scoop out the seeds and discard. Coarsely shred *half* of the cucumber. Thinly slice the remaining half. Cover and refrigerate the sliced cucumber.

For dressing, in a medium mixing bowl stir together the shredded cucumber, sour cream, green onions, wine vinegar, salad oil, dry mustard, and garlic powder. Cover and refrigerate for 2 to 12 hours.

Just before serving, in a salad bowl combine the sliced cucumber and mixed greens. Pour the dressing over the top. Makes 6 servings.

Apple-Berry Ginger Pie

- 1 12-ounce package (3 cups) cranberries
- ¾ cup apple juice
- 1⅓ cups sugar
- ⅓ cup cornstarch
- 3 medium cooking apples, such as McIntosh, Jonathan, *or* Golden Delicious, peeled, cored, and chopped (about 3 cups)
- 1 tablespoon snipped crystallized ginger *or* ½ teaspoon ground ginger
- 1½ cups all-purpose flour
- ½ teaspoon finely shredded orange peel
- ¼ teaspoon salt
- ½ cup shortening
- 4 to 5 tablespoons *cold* water Milk Sifted powdered sugar

For filling, in a medium saucepan cook the cranberries and apple juice, uncovered, over medium heat for 5 to 8 minutes or till cranberries begin to pop, stirring occasionally.

Combine the sugar and the cornstarch. Stir the sugar mixture into the hot cranberry mixture. Cook and stir till thickened and bubbly. Remove saucepan from heat. Stir in the apples and ginger. Set the apple-cranberry filling aside.

For pastry, in a medium mixing bowl stir together the flour, orange peel, and salt. Using a pastry blender, cut in the shortening till pieces are the size of small peas. Sprinkle *1 tablespoon* of the water over part of the mixture, then gently toss with a fork. Push the moistened mixture to the side of the bowl. Repeat, using 1 tablespoon of water at a time, till all of the dough is moistened. Form the dough into a ball.

On a lightly floured surface, use your hands to slightly flatten dough. Roll dough from the center to the edges, forming a circle about 15 inches in diameter. Wrap pastry around the rolling pin. Unroll the pastry onto a 9-inch pie plate. Ease the pastry into the pie plate, being careful not to stretch it. Trim pastry to 1½ to 2 inches beyond edge of the pie plate.

Pour the apple-cranberry filling into the pastry-lined pie plate. Fold the pastry border up over the filling, pleating the pastry to fit. Lightly brush the pastry with milk.

To prevent overbrowning, cover the edge of the pie with foil. Bake in a 375° oven about 15 minutes. Remove foil. Bake for 30 to 35 minutes more or till the pastry is golden. Cool pie on a wire rack. Before serving, sprinkle pie with powdered sugar. Makes 8 servings.

THE SPIRIT OF AN
Elegant Christmas

At the heart of our beloved Christmas traditions stands the evergreen tree, bedecked with glittering ornaments twinkling amidst its boughs. As long ago as 1605, a visitor to Germany wrote of a "Christbaum" decorated with gilt-wrapped candies and paper roses. Recreate this eternal theme of roses and gold by making elegant ornaments and holiday accessories, filling your home with the stuff of which fairy tale dreams are made. Let nature's harvest flow from the decorations to a sumptious buffet table. And everywhere will be the rose, a symbol of the Virgin Mary, to inspire a spirit of romance in all your holiday festivities.

Floss Tassel Ornament

MATERIALS
For one ornament
Three skeins of embroidery floss
Metallic thread (optional)
5-inch square of cardboard
Tapestry needle
Scissors; tape
Plastic soft-toothed hairbrush

INSTRUCTIONS
Note: Metallic threads do not hold up when brushed, so use metallic thread, if desired, only for the hanger loop and the wrapping threads.

Taking nearly equal amounts from each skein, cut eight 10-inch-long floss pieces and one 30-inch length.

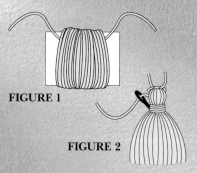

FIGURE 1

FIGURE 2

Wrap the remaining floss around the cardboard. Slip one 10-inch-long piece of floss under the bundle as shown in Figure 1, *above;* tie it tightly around the threads. Remove the tied bundle from the cardboard. Cut the threads opposite the tie.

For the hanging loop, lay six 10-inch-long floss pieces together. Tie the floss together with a knot at one end. Tape the knot to the table.

Twist three threads in your left hand *clockwise* until they are tightly coiled. Twist the remaining threads in your right hand *clockwise* to make another coil. Bring the ends of both coils together; twist *counterclockwise*. Make a knot at the end to secure the spiraled coil. Remove the tape.

Fold the coil in half to make a loop. Tie the last 10-inch-long floss piece tightly around the loop's ends. Cut knots off the hanger loop.

Insert the bundle in the loop, centering the tie of the bundle over the tie of the loop. Smooth the strands of the bundle to hang straight down.

Glitter Ornament

Ornament is approximately 4½ inches in diameter.

MATERIALS
1½-inch-diameter plastic foam ball
250-count box of round toothpicks
10 inches of monofilament thread
Large container of glitter
Newspaper; shallow pan
U-shaped hairpin or paper clip
White crafts glue; spray adhesive

INSTRUCTIONS
Knot the ends of the monofilament to form a loop. Apply glue to both ends of the hairpin; with the loop hanging from the hairpin, push the pin into the foam ball. Let glue dry.

Dip one end of a toothpick in glue, then push it ¼ inch into the foam ball near the loop holder. Continue spacing glue-dipped toothpicks evenly around the ball at ⅛-inch intervals until the ball is covered with toothpicks. Let the glue dry before adding the glitter.

Spread newspaper over a work surface. Working over the newspaper and holding the ball by the loop, spray the ball with adhesive. Holding the ball over a shallow pan, sprinkle glitter over the sticky ball until it is completely covered.

Shake off excess glitter into the pan; hang ball to dry. Reuse glitter in pan to make more ornaments.

Tie the 30-inch-long floss tightly around the bundle 1 inch from the top. Wrap one end of the floss tightly around the bundle, working toward the top; thread this piece of floss into the needle. Insert the needle into the wrapped threads and push it down into the bundle, as shown in Figure 2, *opposite*. Pull the thread taut to secure the wrapping; remove the needle.

Wrap the other end of the thread over the first wrapping. Thread the needle with the last 8 inches. Insert the needle into the bottom of the wrapping; bring it out through the top of the bundle. Wrap the floss tightly around the bottom of the hanger loop, then insert the needle into this wrapping and down into the bundle. Remove the needle. Trim the bottom of the tassel even.

Use the hairbrush to gently brush and separate the strands of the floss.

Doily Ornament

MATERIALS
6-inch-diameter purchased
    crocheted ecru doily
Fabric stiffening solution
Small silk flowers and leaves
Assorted beads, charms, buttons,
    and ribbon roses
7-inch ribbon or thread hanger
Hot-glue gun; extra glue sticks
White crafts glue
Clothespins
Plastic bag; waxed paper
Purple and magenta fabric spray
    paints (optional)

INSTRUCTIONS
Put the doily in a plastic bag with approximately 1 cup of stiffening solution. Massage the solution thoroughly into the doily. Remove doily, squeezing the excess solution from it.

Lay the doily on waxed paper; ripple and scrunch the doily into the size and shape that you want. Leave the doily in place on the waxed paper until it hardens and is completely dry.

Paint the silk flowers with fabric spray paint, if desired. Let paint dry before gluing flowers to the doily.

Cut flowers from stems. Hot-glue selected leaves, flowers, and ribbon roses onto the stiffened doily. Use white crafts glue to glue beads, buttons, and charms to the doily, filling in empty places between flowers.

For a hanger, loop 7 inches of ribbon or thread through an opening in the doily's crocheted edge. Knot the loop ends to secure the hanger.

Hearts and Bows Cross-Stitched Stockings

Finished stocking is approximately 14½ inches long. Stitch count is 126 wide and 200 high.

MATERIALS

14x20-inch piece of 14-count Damask Aida cloth
One skein of embroidery floss for each color listed in the color key on page 32
1 yard of rose fabric for lining, back, and piping
1½ yards of ¼-inch-diameter cotton cording for piping
1¼ yards of ⅜-inch-wide satin ribbon and five purchased rosettes for partially stitched stocking only

INSTRUCTIONS

Following the chart on pages 32 and 33, center and stitch the stocking design on the Damask Aida. Referring to the photo, *opposite*, decide whether to stitch the allover design or just the top portion of the design. Use three strands of floss for cross-stitches and one strand for backstitches.

Using the charted alphabet, *right*, center and stitch a name in the designated area at the stocking top. The lower line on the chart is the baseline for a capital letter; the higher line is the baseline for lowercase letters.

Hand-sew running stitches around the perimeter of the stitchery to outline the stocking shape. Trim the Aida cloth ½ inch beyond the running stitches. Using the trimmed piece as a pattern, trace and cut three stocking shapes from the rose fabric for the stocking back and lining.

From the remaining rose fabric, cut and piece three 1½-inch-wide bias strips. Make one strip 38 inches long; a second strip 14¼ inches, and a third strip 5½ inches long. Use the two longer strips and the cording to make piping.

Baste the longest piece of piping around the stocking on the right side of the fabric, matching raw edges.

With right sides together, sew the stocking back to the front, leaving the top edge open. Clip curves; turn right side out. Check to see that piping is sewn neatly into the seam.

continued

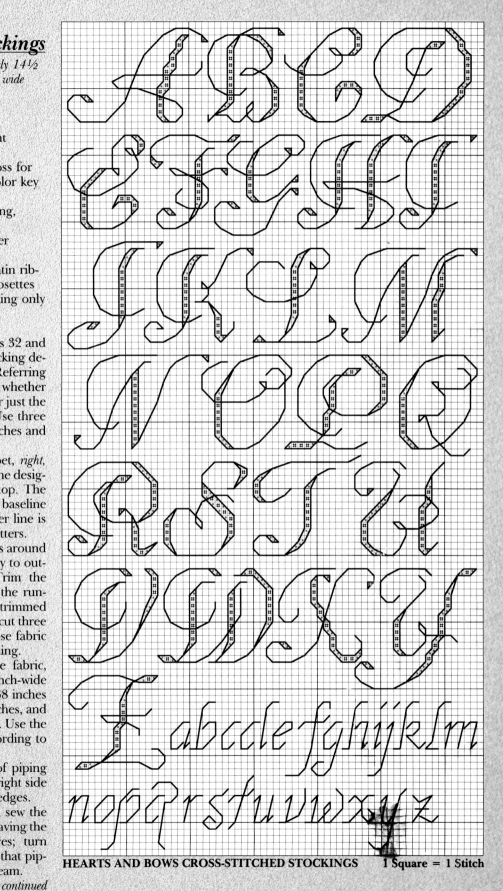

HEARTS AND BOWS CROSS-STITCHED STOCKINGS   **1 Square = 1 Stitch**

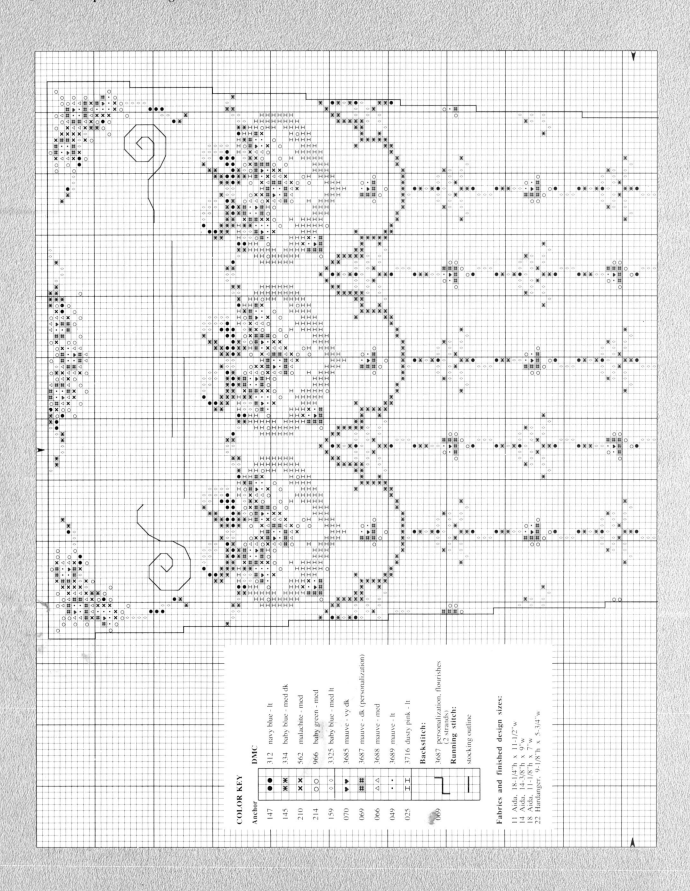

COLOR KEY									
Anchor	DMC								
147	312	navy blue - lt	●	✳					
145	334	baby blue - med dk	●	✳	✖				
210	562	malachite - med		✖	○				
214	966	baby green - med	▶		○				
159	3325	baby blue - lt		✳	▶				
070	3685	mauve - vy dk			▶	#			
069	3687	mauve - dk (personalization)				#	△		
066	3688	mauve - med					△		
049	3689	mauve - lt					•	•	
025	3716	dusty pink - lt						Ⅱ	Ⅰ

Backstitch:

069   3687   personalization, flourishes
(2 strands)

Running stitch:

stocking outline

Fabrics and finished design sizes:

11 Aida, 18-1/4"h x 11-1/2"w
14 Aida, 14-3/8"h x 9"w
18 Aida, 11-1/8"h x 7"w
22 Hardanger, 9-1/8"h x 5-3/4"w

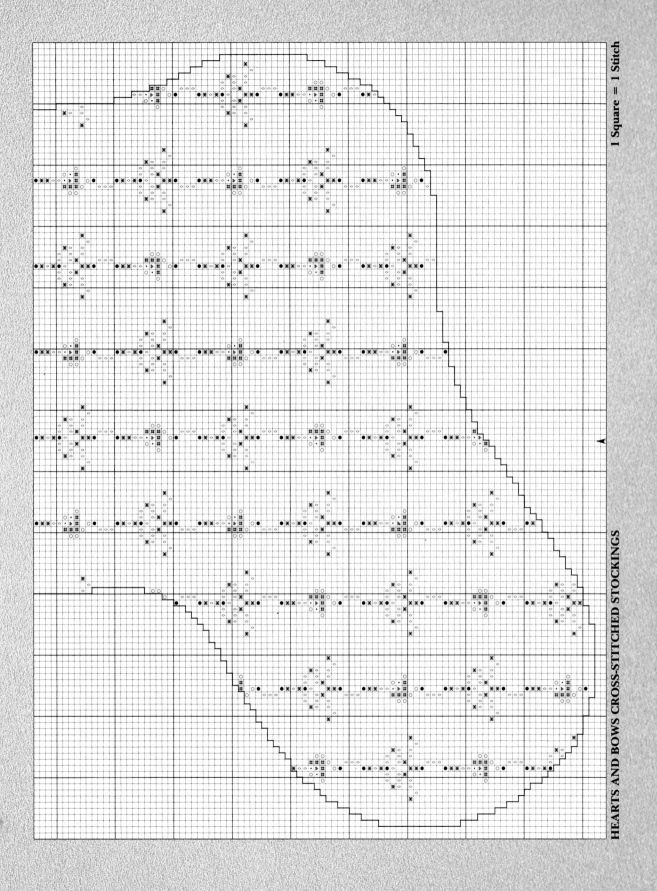

HEARTS AND BOWS CROSS-STITCHED STOCKINGS

Baste the 14¼-inch strip of piping around the top of the stocking on the right side, overlapping the piping ends at the center back.

Fold the 5½-inch-long bias strip in half lengthwise. Machine-stitch a generous ¼ inch from the fold. Trim seam allowance; turn to right side and press. Matching raw edges, tack the ends of the strip to the top right corner of the stocking back.

Using a ½-inch seam allowance, machine-stitch lining pieces together around sides and foot; leave a 6-inch opening in one side. Trim seam allowance to ¼ inch; clip curves. Do not turn lining.

With right sides together, slip the stocking inside of lining. Sew the two units together around the top edge of the stocking. Trim seam; turn stocking right side out. Slip-stitch opening in lining; insert lining into stocking.

Sew ribbon bows and rosettes onto stocking front as desired.

Ribbon-Rose Ornament

MATERIALS
For one rose
30- to 42-inch-long piece of
  1½-inch-wide wire-edged ribbon
  in desired color
Two 6-inch-long pieces of
  1-inch-wide green wire-edged
  ribbon for leaves
Coordinating thread and sewing
  needle

INSTRUCTIONS
Pull the wire out of one edge of the ribbon; work with this edge on the bottom of the rose. Have a threaded needle ready, with a knot in the end of the thread, before you begin to wrap the ribbon. Save the removed wire to finish the rose.

To form the rose center, tightly roll one end of the ribbon for about 1½ inches. Hand-sew the bottom edges tightly to secure the cylinder.

Holding the rolled end in one hand, use your other hand to loosely wrap the remaining ribbon around the center. As the rose grows, gather the bottom edges, basting them in place with each turn around the center. Shape the top edges as desired (the wire edge will hold the shape).

FIGURE 1

At the end of the ribbon, fold in the raw edge and baste. Tie off the thread at the bottom of the rose.

Tie a 12-inch-long piece of the removed wire around the bottom of the rose. Wrap part of the wire tightly around the rose; use the wire ends to attach the rose ornament to the tree.

Fold a piece of green ribbon as shown in Figure 1, *above*, and Figure 2 at *right*. Gather the raw edges at the bottom of the ribbon as shown in Figure 3, *right*; secure gathers. Use the excess thread from the gathering to sew the leaf to the bottom of the rose. Make two leaves for each rose.

FIGURE 2

FIGURE 3

Ribbon-Rose Tree Skirt

MATERIALS
70-inch-diameter lace tablecloth
44 to 50 ribbon roses with leaves
  (see instructions, *opposite*)
12 feet *each* of green paper twist
  and florist's wire
Aluminum foil
Low-temperature glue gun

INSTRUCTIONS
Cut a 10-inch diameter circle in the center of the tablecloth, then cut a slit from the center out to the edge of the cloth; hem the cut edges.

Wrap florist's wire loosely around the paper twist. With the cloth lying flat atop a sheet of foil, arrange the paper twist around the outer edge in undulating curves. Glue the twist in place as you work around the cloth, holding each segment in place until the glue is dry enough to stick.

Cut the remaining twist into 8- to 10-inch lengths; glue these in place as branches between the curves of the vine. Glue roses and leaves in place as desired. When glue is dry, pull the stuck foil away from the cloth.

Nosegay Tree Topper

MATERIALS
Three ribbon roses with leaves (see instructions, *opposite*)
One 10-inch-diameter paper doily with plastic cone center (available at many crafts shops, florists, and bridal suppliers)
Three 14-inch-long pieces of wire
Gold spray paint

INSTRUCTIONS
Spray doily with gold paint; let dry before adding roses.

Wrap one end of a 14-inch-long piece of the ribbon wire around the bottom of each rose. Push the remaining wire end through the opening in the doily cone.

Wrap wire ends around the top of the tree to secure the nosegay. Add ribbon streamers as desired.

Ivy Tree Topiary

MATERIALS
For one topiary
8 to 10 ivy plants
Potting soil
Terra-cotta pot; sphagnum moss
Chicken wire; wire cutters
Plaster of paris; straight hairpins
½-inch-diameter (or larger)
  wooden dowel of desired length
Paper, compass, protractor, pencil
Ribbon and ribbon roses as desired

INSTRUCTIONS
Mix plaster according to package directions; fill flowerpot with plaster. Insert dowel in center before plaster sets. For each topiary, use a dowel 6 inches *longer* than the radius of the pattern circle made in the next step.

On paper, draw a circle with a radius equal to the desired height of one topiary. (The topiaries shown are 26 inches, 30 inches, and 36 inches tall.) Use the protractor to divide the circle into three equal sections as shown at

right. Cut out one section for a pattern, then cut the pattern shape out of chicken wire.

Join the edges to form a cone; twist the wire to secure the edges.

Stand the cone atop another sheet of chicken wire and cut a circle of wire to fit the base. Twist wire edges to secure base to the cone. Centering the base over the dowel, push the cone down to rest on top of the pot.

Open the cone seam to push wet moss into the tip and atop the base. Fill the interior with soil, then twist the wire together again. Push ivy plants through the wire into the soil.

Mist plants daily until ivy is established, then as needed. Train ivy to conform with wire shape as it grows, securing tendrils with hairpins.

Allow 12 weeks to grow ivy over a medium-size topiary. For the holidays, decorate the topiary as desired.

Decorated Birdcage

MATERIALS
Wire birdcage
Six to eight small artificial birds
Hot-glue gun
Burgundy spray paint
Spanish moss
Grapevine
Dried flowers and naturals such as
  pepperberries, ground cherries,
  pink daisies, and small pinecones

INSTRUCTIONS
Lightly dust the ground cherries with burgundy spray paint; let dry.

Weave strands of grapevine between and around the wires of the cage. Make a nest of Spanish moss among the vines at the bottom of the birdcage.

Position the birds on the grapevine; secure with wire and/or glue.

Use the glue gun to secure remaining dried materials to the cage wires and grapevine as desired.

Dried-Flower Wreath And Centerpiece With a Touch of Gold

MATERIALS

Assorted naturals including thistle
  flower, pepperberries, amaranth,
  pepperweed, statice, pennycress,
  milkweed flower, and pinecones
Cattails for the centerpiece
Purchased 24-inch-diameter wire
  form for the wreath
22-gauge wire
Chicken wire
⅛-inch-wide metallic gold soutache
  or cording
1-inch-wide wire-edged ribbon in
  desired color
Spray paint in desired color
Gold-leaf paint; small paintbrush
White crafts glue; wire cutters
Felt to cover bottom of centerpiece
  (optional)

INSTRUCTIONS

Preparing the naturals

To add a touch of gold to the pinecones, apply a little gold-leaf paint to
the tips. Cut a 12-inch-long piece of
wire for each pinecone; wrap one end
of the wire around the bottom of the
pinecone, leaving a tail of wire approximately 7 inches long.

Give the pepperweed and pennycress a hint of color with a light dust-
ing of spray paint.

Assembling the wreath

Cover the wreath form with a wrapping of chicken wire.

Use pepperweed and pennycress
to make a base for the other naturals.
Starting at the outside and working
toward the center, poke stems of
pepperweed and pennycress into the
wire until the wreath form is nearly
covered. Fill in with other dried flowers, gluing them in place. Weave gold
soutache or cording in and out as the
arrangement takes shape.

To add pinecones, push the wires
through the chicken wire to the back
of the form; wrap the wire tails
around the wire form to secure the
pinecones. Add a bow of colored ribbon in the same manner.

Assembling the centerpiece

Make a base from chicken wire by
cutting one 4x10-inch piece and one
6x12-inch piece. Roll the smaller
piece into a tight 2x4-inch cylinder;
secure it with a wire tie, if necessary.
Roll the remaining piece of chicken
wire loosely around the first cylinder.

Push cattail stems into the wire,
positioning them as desired. Next,
pull clumps of pepperweed through
the holes in the outer base to form a
base of dried flowers.

Glue remaining flowers onto the
base as desired. Wire the pinecones
and bow in place as for the wreath.

To protect your tabletop from exposed chicken wire, glue felt to the
bottom of the finished centerpiece.

Madonna and Child Scherenschnitte

MATERIALS

Good quality 8½x11-inch bond
   paper or parchment in desired
   color for scherenschnitte
Tracing paper
Graphite paper, available at art and
   crafts stores; sharp pencil
Mat board for mounting design
Sharp 4-inch embroidery or
   manicure scissors
Stapler or tape; crafts glue

INSTRUCTIONS

Trace the pattern, *opposite,* onto tracing paper. Staple the corners of the
graphite and traced-design papers
atop the scherenschnitte paper with
the traced pattern faceup and the carbon side of the graphite paper facing
the scherenschnitte paper.

With a sharp pencil, retrace the
drawing. Go over every line only
once for proper registration. When
drawing is complete, remove staples
and separate the scherenschnitte paper from the others.

Begin to cut the inside areas of the
design first, working out toward the
outer edges of the circle. This leaves
a larger area to hold onto while cutting the tiny inside openings. Always
cut with the tips of the scissors, completely closing the tips at the end of
each snip.

Apply tiny dabs of glue to the back
of the design to adhere it to the mat
board. If desired, place a sheet of
glass atop the design to hold the paper flat against the mat.

Frame as desired.

MADONNA AND CHILD SCHERENSCHNITTE PATTERN

ROMANTIC
Christmas Brunch

Candlelight, lace coverings, and crystal so bright, bring forth a sparkling setting for an elegant celebration featuring morning foods.

Romantic Christmas Brunch

Cranberry Wassail

Scrambled Egg Casserole

Turkey-Apple Sausages

Steamed asparagus spears

Miniature Caramel-Pecan Rolls or Gingerbread Scones

Miniature English muffins or toast points

Butter curls, assorted marmalades and jams, and lemon or raspberry curd

Poached Peaches and Grapes or Poached Fruit in Zinfandel

Timetable

Up to 3 months ahead

Prepare and bake Gingerbread Scones. Freeze.

1 day ahead

Prepare the Cranberry Wassail and Poached Peaches and Grapes or Poached Fruit in Zinfandel. Also, prepare, but do not bake, the Scrambled Egg Casserole, Turkey-Apple Sausages, and Miniature Caramel-Pecan Rolls. Refrigerate each.

2 hours ahead

Let the Miniature Caramel-Pecan Rolls stand at room temperature for 20 minutes, then bake.

45 minutes ahead

Bake the Scrambled Egg Casserole and Turkey-Apple Sausages. Steam the asparagus spears. Toast English muffins or make toast points. Reheat the Cranberry Wassail and Gingerbread Scones.

Cranberry Wassail

- 1 **32-ounce jar cranberry juice cocktail**
- 1 **cup water**
- ½ **of a 6-ounce can (⅓ cup) frozen pineapple-orange juice concentrate, thawed**
- 6 **inches stick cinnamon**
- 2 **whole cloves**
  Orange peel strips (optional)
  Stick cinnamon (optional)

♠ In a large saucepan stir together the cranberry juice cocktail, water, pineapple-orange juice concentrate, the 6 inches stick cinnamon, and cloves. Bring to boiling; reduce heat. Cover and simmer for 10 minutes.

♠ Using a slotted spoon, remove cinnamon and cloves from juice mixture. Transfer the juice mixture to a container. Cool slightly. Cover and refrigerate for up to 7 days.

♠ To reheat the juice mixture, transfer it to a large saucepan and heat till warm. Carefully pour into a heatproof punch bowl. Ladle juice into cups and, if desired, garnish with orange peel strips tied around stick cinnamon. Makes 10 (4½-ounce) servings.

Scrambled Egg Casserole

- ½ **cup sliced green onion *or* chopped green pepper**
- 6 **tablespoons margarine *or* butter**
- 12 **beaten eggs**
- 2 **tablespoons all-purpose flour**
- ¼ **teaspoon pepper**
- 1⅓ **cups milk**
- 1½ **cups shredded American *or* process Swiss cheese (6 ounces)**
- ¼ **cup diced pimiento**
- ½ **cup fine dry plain *or* seasoned bread crumbs**

♣ In a large skillet cook the onion or green pepper in *2 tablespoons* of the margarine till tender. Pour the eggs into the skillet. Cook, without stirring, over medium heat till mixture begins to set on bottom and around edge. Then, using a large spoon or spatula, lift and fold the partially cooked eggs so the uncooked portion flows underneath. Continue cooking over medium heat about 3 minutes or till eggs are cooked throughout but are still glossy and moist. *Immediately* transfer eggs to a 1½-quart casserole or a 10x6x2-inch baking dish. Set eggs aside.

♣ For sauce, in a small saucepan melt *2 tablespoons* of the margarine. Stir in flour and pepper. Add milk all at once. Cook and stir till thickened and bubbly. Stir in cheese and cook just till melted. Stir in pimiento. Pour sauce over cooked eggs and gently stir together till eggs are coated. Cover and refrigerate for 3 to 24 hours.

♣ Bake the egg mixture, covered, in a 350° oven for 25 minutes. Uncover the casserole or baking dish and bake about 25 minutes more or till hot.

♣ Meanwhile, in a medium skillet melt the remaining margarine or butter. Add the bread crumbs. Cook and stir over medium heat about 2 minutes or till crumbs are toasted. To serve, transfer eggs to a serving bowl. Sprinkle with toasted bread crumbs. Makes 8 servings.

Turkey-Apple Sausages

    1 **slightly beaten egg**
    ½ **cup soft bread crumbs**
    ½ **cup finely chopped, peeled apple**
    ½ **teaspoon salt**
    ½ **teaspoon ground sage**
    ¼ **teaspoon pepper**
    1 **pound ground raw turkey *or* lean ground beef *or* pork**
       Apple peel roses (optional)
       Fresh sage (optional)

♣ In a medium mixing bowl combine the egg, bread crumbs, chopped apple, salt, ground sage, and pepper. Add the ground turkey, beef, or pork and mix well.

♣ Shape the turkey mixture into 16 small patties, about 2½ inches in diameter. Cover and refrigerate the sausage patties for 3 to 24 hours.

♣ To cook sausage patties, place them on a rack in a shallow baking pan. Bake in a 350° oven for 15 to 20 minutes or till no longer pink. If necessary, pat the patties with paper towels to remove excess fat.

♣ To serve, arrange the sausage patties on a platter. If desired, garnish with apple peel roses and fresh sage. Makes 8 servings.

Miniature Caramel-Pecan Rolls

    4¼ **to 4¾ cups all-purpose flour**
     1 **package active dry yeast**
     1 **cup milk**
     ⅓ **cup sugar**
     ⅓ **cup margarine *or* butter**
     ½ **teaspoon salt**
     2 **eggs**
     ⅓ **cup margarine *or* butter**
     ⅔ **cup packed brown sugar**
     2 **tablespoons light corn syrup**
     1 **cup broken pecans**
     ¼ **cup margarine *or* butter, melted**
     ½ **cup sugar**
     1 **teaspoon ground cinnamon**

♣ For dough, in a large mixing bowl stir together *1½ cups* of the flour and the yeast; set aside. In a medium saucepan heat and stir the milk, the ⅓ cup sugar, ⅓ cup margarine or butter, and salt *just till warm* (120° to 130°) and the margarine or butter almost melts. Add the milk mixture to the flour mixture. Then add eggs. Beat with an electric mixer on low to medium

speed for 30 seconds, scraping the sides of the bowl. Beat on high speed for 3 minutes. Using a wooden spoon, stir in as much of the remaining flour as you can.

♣ Turn the dough out onto a lightly floured surface. Knead in enough of the remaining flour to make a moderately soft dough that is smooth and elastic (3 to 5 minutes total). Shape the dough into a ball. Place dough in a lightly greased bowl, turning once to grease the surface of the dough. Cover and let dough rise in a warm place till double in size (about 1 hour).

♣ Punch dough down. Turn out onto a lightly floured surface. Divide in half. Cover and let rest for 10 minutes.

♣ Meanwhile, in a small saucepan melt ⅓ cup margarine or butter. Stir in the brown sugar and the corn syrup. Cook and stir *just till blended*. Pour the syrup mixture evenly in the bottom of a 15½x10½x2-inch baking pan. *Or*, divide the syrup mixture between two 9x9x2-inch baking pans or one 13x9x2-inch baking pan and one 8x8x2-inch baking pan. Sprinkle the broken pecans over the syrup. Set pan(s) aside.

♣ Divide *each* half of the dough in half. On a lightly floured surface, roll *each* portion of dough into a 12x6-inch rectangle. Brush the ¼ cup melted margarine or butter on top of the dough and sprinkle with a mixture of the ½ cup sugar and the cinnamon.

♣ Roll up each rectangle, jelly-roll style, starting from one of the long sides. Pinch seams to seal. Cut *each* roll into *twelve* 1-inch pieces. Place pieces cut sides down in the prepared pan. Cover rolls with oiled waxed paper, then with plastic wrap. Refrigerate the unbaked rolls for 2 to 24 hours.

♣ Before baking the rolls, let them stand, covered, for 20 minutes at room temperature. Using a greased toothpick, puncture any surface bubbles on the rolls. Bake in a 375° oven for 20 to 25 minutes or till tops are golden. Invert the rolls onto wire racks. Cool slightly, then serve. Makes 48.

Gingerbread Scones

2¼ cups all-purpose flour
¼ cup packed brown sugar
2 teaspoons baking powder
1 teaspoon ground ginger
½ teaspoon ground cinnamon
¼ teaspoon baking soda
¼ teaspoon ground cloves
⅓ cup *cold* margarine *or* butter
1 beaten egg
¼ cup molasses
2 tablespoons milk
¾ cup mixed dried fruit bits *or* light raisins

♠ In a large mixing bowl stir together the flour, brown sugar, baking powder, ginger, cinnamon, baking soda, and cloves. Using a pastry blender, cut in the margarine or butter till the mixture resembles coarse crumbs. Make a well in the center of the dry mixture.

♠ In a small mixing bowl stir together the beaten egg, molasses, and milk. Add the egg mixture all at once to the dry mixture. Using a fork, stir *just till well combined.* Stir in the fruit bits or raisins.

♠ Turn the dough out onto a lightly floured surface. Quickly knead the dough by gently folding and pressing it for 10 to 12 strokes or till the dough is *nearly* smooth. Divide the dough in half.

♠ On an ungreased baking sheet, pat or lightly roll *each* dough portion into a 6-inch circle. Using a sharp knife, cut *each* circle into *6* wedges. Separate wedges by pulling them 1 inch apart from each other.

♠ Bake scones in a 375° oven for 12 to 15 minutes or till tops look dry and a wooden toothpick inserted near the center of each scone comes out clean. Remove scones from baking sheet. Cool slightly on a wire rack, then serve warm. *Or,* cool completely before freezing. Makes 12.

To freeze: Wrap the scones in *heavy* foil. Seal, label, and freeze them for up to 3 months. To thaw and serve, reheat the frozen, wrapped scones in a 350° oven for 15 to 20 minutes or till warm.

Poached Peaches and Grapes

1 orange
1½ cups water
⅔ cup sugar
1 tablespoon vanilla
2 16-ounce packages frozen unsweetened peach slices *or* 6 medium nectarines, pitted and sliced
1½ cups seedless red *and/or* green grapes, halved
Fresh mint (optional)

♠ Using a vegetable peeler or a small sharp knife, remove *two* 2x1-inch thin strips of peel from the orange. Leave the bitter white membrane attached to the orange flesh, not to the peel. (Reserve the orange for another use.)

♠ For the syrup, in a large saucepan stir together the water, sugar, and vanilla. Add the orange peel strips. Bring to boiling, stirring till sugar is dissolved.

♠ Add the frozen peaches or nectarines to the syrup mixture. Return to boiling. Reduce heat. Cover and simmer for 3 to 5 minutes or till fruit is *just tender.* Remove saucepan from heat.

♠ Transfer the peaches and syrup to a bowl. Remove orange peel strips and stir in grapes. Cool slightly. If desired, cover and refrigerate for up to 24 hours.

♠ Serve the warm or chilled fruit mixture and its syrup in 8 wine glasses or dessert dishes. If desired, garnish each serving with a mint sprig. Makes 8 servings.

Poached Fruit in Zinfandel

16 (8 ounces) dried Calimyrna figs
3 cups water
1 cup dried cherries, dried cranberries, *or* raisins
4 oranges
2 cups white zinfandel wine
¾ cup sugar
½ cup orange liqueur
10 cardamom pods, opened
Whipped cream (optional)
Fresh mint (optional)
Orange peel curls (optional)

♠ Remove the stems from the figs. Cut each fig into quarters. In a medium saucepan combine the figs; water; and cherries, cranberries, or raisins. Bring mixture to boiling. Remove from heat and let stand for 20 minutes. Drain off liquid.

♠ Using a sharp knife, remove the peel and bitter white membrane from the oranges. If desired, reserve the peel and make orange peel curls for garnish. Cut the oranges crosswise into ½-inch-thick slices. Cut each orange slice into quarters. In a large bowl combine the oranges and the fig-cherry mixture; set aside.

♠ For syrup, in the medium saucepan stir together the wine, sugar, and orange liqueur. Place the seeds from the cardamom pods in the center of a 6-inch square of 100 percent cotton cheesecloth. Bring up the corners of the cheesecloth and tie them with a clean string. Add the cardamom bag to the wine mixture. Heat and stir wine mixture till sugar is dissolved. Then bring the mixture to boiling. Boil gently, uncovered, for 20 minutes or till slightly thickened. Remove saucepan from heat and remove and discard the cardamom bag.

♠ Pour the hot syrup mixture over the fruit in the large bowl. Gently stir till fruit is coated. Cool slightly. Cover and refrigerate for 4 to 24 hours.

♠ To serve, spoon the chilled fruit mixture and its syrup into 8 wine glasses or dessert dishes. If desired, garnish each serving with whipped cream, a mint sprig, and an orange peel curl. Makes 8 servings.

GLORY TO THE
Newborn King

"*And there were in the
same country shepherds
abiding in the field, keeping
watch over their flock by
night. And, lo, the angel of
the Lord came upon them,
and the glory of the Lord
shone round about them
and they were sore afraid.
And the angel said unto
them, 'Fear not, for behold,
I bring you tidings of great
joy, which shall be to all
people. For unto you is
born this day in the city of
David a Saviour, which is
Christ the Lord. And this
shall be a sign unto you; ye
shall find the babe wrapped
in swaddling clothes, lying
in a manger.'*" Luke II: 8–12

Wooden Nativity Set

Stable measures 12 inches wide, 9 inches deep, and 8¾ inches high. Figurines range from 1½ to 4½ inches tall.

MATERIALS

Scraps or a 1x8x48-inch piece of clear white pine for the stable

6x24 inches of ⁵⁄₄-inch clear white pine for figurines and manger

Carpenter's wood glue

Five No. 8 flathead wood screws

7 inches of ¼-inch-diameter wooden dowel to assemble the posts and beams

7 inches of ⅛-inch copper wire or 5-inch-long wooden dowel for the shepherd's staff

Coarse- and fine-grit sandpaper

No. 8 and No. 0 paintbrushes

Liquitex acrylic paints in the colors listed in the color key on page 53, or colors of your choice

Metallic gold paint for trim

Warm-brown stain for stable

Acrylic spray sealer

Spray satin-finish varnish

Wood excelsior for manger straw

Band saw or jigsaw

Table saw with dado blade

Drill with ¼-, ⅛-, ⅜-, and ³⁄₃₂-inch drill bits

Screwdriver; clamps

Tracing paper; carbon paper

INSTRUCTIONS

Note: Throughout these instructions, refer to the diagrams on page 51 to identify the stable parts by letter designation and to the Bill of Materials on page 50 for size and quantity required of each part.

Preparation of materials for the stable

For the base (A), cut one piece of pine ¾x7x12 inches.

Drill ⁵⁄₃₂-inch holes ½ inch in from each corner of the base. Drill a fifth hole halfway between the two holes along the back edge. Countersink each hole on the bottom for a No. 8 flathead wood screw.

For the support posts (B), cut one piece of pine ¾x4½x7¾ inches.

continued

Referring to the Forming the Posts diagram, *right,* cut a dado in one end of this wood stock. First, set up a ¼-inch-wide dado blade on the table saw. Position the fence ¼ inch from the inside edge of the dado blade. Rip a slot ¼x¾ inch deep along the bottom edge of the wood. Rip the stock into five ¾-inch-wide posts (B).

Cut two ¾x¾x12¼-inch pieces for the cross beams (C).

Referring to the Slot and Tenon Detail diagram, *opposite, upper right,* mark dado and tenon locations on both beams. Set a ¾-inch dado blade on your table saw. Crosscut ¾-inch dadoes ¼ inch deep in the center of each side of the rear beam. Cut tenons ¼x1 inch long on the ends of both beams. Sand ¼ inch off corners of beam tenons at a 45-degree angle.

For the corner braces (D), cut two ¾x¾x2½-inch pine pieces. Crosscut both ends of the two braces at a 45-degree angle.

To cut wooden slats for the back, sides, and roof (E, F, and G) from a ¾x4x36-inch stock, set up a fence with a ¼-inch gap between fence and blade on your band saw. Rip the 4-inch-wide board into eleven ¼-inch strips. The band saw is used to give strips a rough look. Crosscut these strips for E's, F's, and G's as listed in the Bill of Materials, *below.*

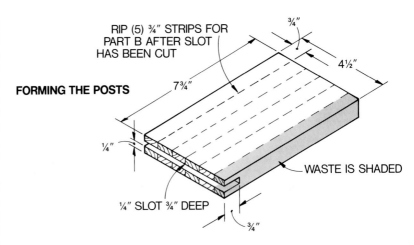

RIP (5) ¾" STRIPS FOR PART B AFTER SLOT HAS BEEN CUT

FORMING THE POSTS

¾"

4½"

7¾"

¼"

WASTE IS SHADED

¼" SLOT ¾" DEEP

¾"

Bill of Materials

Part	Finished Size			Qty.
	T	W	L	
A Base	¾"	7"	12"	1
B Post	¾"	¾"	7¾"	5
C Cross Beam	¾"	¾"	12¼"	2
D Corner Brace	¾"	¾"	2½"	2
E Back Slat	¼"	¾"	11¾"	9
F Side Slat	¼"	¾"	6¼"	14
G Roof Slat	¼"	¾"	9"	16

Assembling the stable

Refer to the assembly diagram, *opposite,* to join pieces as described in the following instructions.

Place each B piece onto A. Note that the B pieces sit ⅛ inch in from the edge of A. Drill ⁷⁄₆₄-inch pilot holes through the shank holes in the bottom of A up ¾ inch into B pieces.

Screw B pieces to A with wood screws. *Do not glue B pieces to A yet.*

Slip C's onto B's. Referring to the Slot and Tenon Detail diagram, drill ¼-inch holes through B's into C's.

Crosscut the 7-inch dowel into five 1¼-inch-long dowels. Sand a slight chamfer on the edges of each dowel segment.

Remove C's from B's; apply a little glue to slots, dadoes, and tenons. Fit B's and C's back together. Apply glue to B and C holes; drive dowels into holes, leaving ¼ inch of each dowel protruding from B's. Sand a dowel slightly if it won't go into a hole. Let the glue dry.

Unscrew B's from A; apply glue to bottom of B's and screw B's onto A.

Turn stable on its top; referring to the Brace Detail diagram, *opposite, lower left,* glue and nail the D corner braces to B's and C's.

Upend the stable onto one side. Apply a dot of glue to each end of the seven side slats (F). Place the slats evenly between the B posts, spacing them approximately ⅛ inch apart. Clamp or weight the slats until the glue is dry. *Note:* Don't worry about getting the slats perfectly parallel; if getting the slats perfectly parallel; if

they are slightly out of alignment, the stable will have a more rustic look.

Glue side slats on the opposite side of the stable in the same manner.

Place stable on front. Apply a thin line of glue on the back of each of the three B posts, starting at the bottom and stopping 1 inch from the top. Place all the back slats (E's) onto B's. Butt each slat up against the other. Clamp or weight these slats until the glue is dry.

With the stable right side up, apply a thin line of glue along the length of each C beam. Place the roof slats (G's) vertically between the beams to form the roof. Roof slats hang 1¾ inches past the front beam and start ⅛ inch from the ends of the tenons on each side. Clamp or weight the roof slats until the glue is dry.

STAINING: Clean all dirt and sawdust from the stable. Stain according to the manufacturer's directions; let dry. Apply several coats of varnish.

Cutting the figurines

Trace patterns for the figurines on pages 52 and 53 onto tracing paper. Place your traced patterns and a piece of carbon paper on the ⁵⁄₄-inch pine; transfer just the outlines of the figurines onto the wood. Aligning the marked arrows on the patterns with the wood grain will ensure that you have enough wood for all figurines.

Cut out all pieces with a jigsaw or band saw. Cut the baby to ½ inch thick. Sand all surfaces; round edges except for bases.

continued

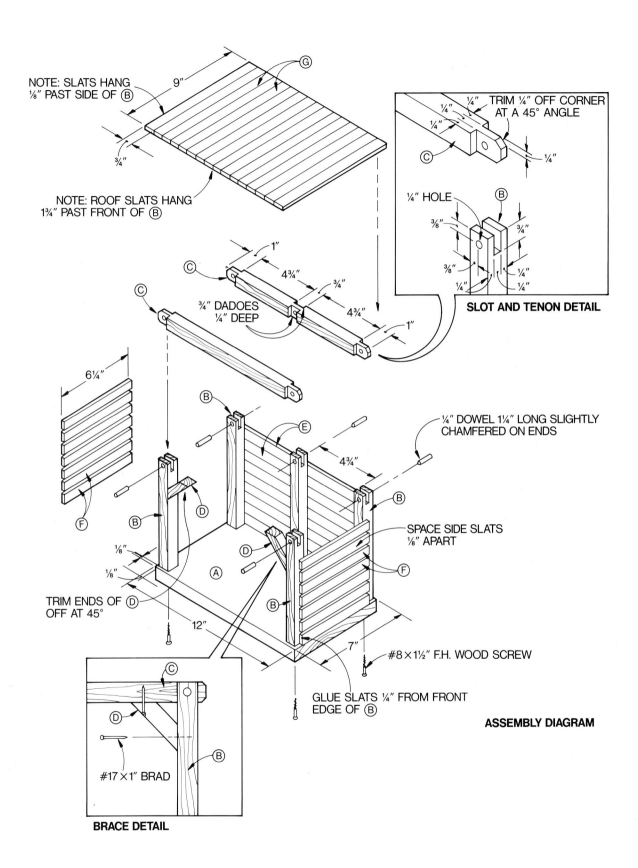

NOTE: SLATS HANG
⅛" PAST SIDE OF Ⓑ

9"

Ⓖ

¾"

NOTE: ROOF SLATS HANG
1¾" PAST FRONT OF Ⓑ

TRIM ¼" OFF CORNER
AT A 45° ANGLE
¼"
¼"
¼"
¼"
Ⓒ

¼" HOLE
⅜"
¾"
Ⓑ
⅜"
¼"
¼"
¼"

SLOT AND TENON DETAIL

Ⓒ
1"
4¾"
¾"
Ⓒ
¾" DADOES
¼" DEEP
4¾"
1"

6¼"

Ⓑ
Ⓔ

¼" DOWEL 1¼" LONG SLIGHTLY
CHAMFERED ON ENDS

4¾"

Ⓑ

Ⓑ
Ⓓ
Ⓕ
Ⓑ

SPACE SIDE SLATS
⅛" APART

⅛"
⅛"

Ⓓ
Ⓐ
Ⓕ

TRIM ENDS OF Ⓓ
OFF AT 45°

12"
Ⓑ

7"

#8×1½" F.H. WOOD SCREW

GLUE SLATS ¼" FROM FRONT
EDGE OF Ⓑ

ASSEMBLY DIAGRAM

Ⓒ
Ⓓ
Ⓑ

#17×1" BRAD

BRACE DETAIL

Trace and cut out the 2½x2-inch manger. Set the manger on its end; trace the end view lines as illustrated *opposite, far right*. Cut out the center; angle-trim the sides using the band saw. Sand until smooth.

Painting and staining the figurines

Seal all sides of figurines except the baby with acrylic spray. On the baby, seal the top and sides only and mark an X on the bottom to identify it.

Stain outside and ends of manger only to match the stable (*do not stain or seal the center*). Next, seal outside and ends of manger with acrylic spray.

After sealer is dry on all figurines, re-sand with fine-grit sandpaper.

Drill one ⅛-inch hole vertically through the shepherd's extended arm. Referring to the staff pattern, *left*, bend copper wire to shape. Or use a ⅛-inch wooden dowel to make a straight staff. Push the staff through the hole in the shepherd's arm from top to bottom until it is even with bottom of shepherd.

Trace face and clothing details onto each figurine. Paint each figurine as indicated by the color key, *opposite*, or decorate as desired.

To make Mix No. 1, combine equal parts of titanium white and bronze yellow. For Mix No. 2, mix burnt sienna with small quantities of titanium white and mars black. Make Mix No. 3 by adding a little phthalocyanine green to turquoise green.

Referring to the photograph on pages 48 and 49 and the patterns, add finer details such as mouths, eyes, hands, and gold trims; let dry. Paint bottoms of each figurine except the baby.

Spread glue inside the manger. Crunch up the wood excelsior; press a small amount into manger. Put glue on the bottom of the baby, then press it into the excelsior. Wrap a strong rubber band several times around manger and baby; dry overnight.

Apply one coat of polyurethane to all figurines, the baby, and manger.

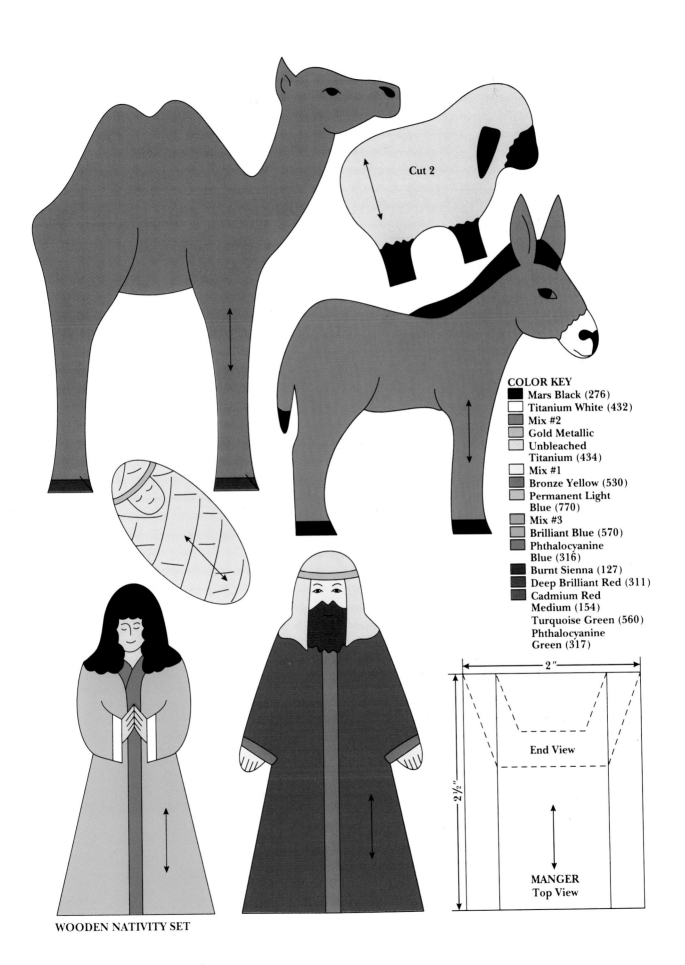

Cut 2

COLOR KEY
- Mars Black (276)
- Titanium White (432)
- Mix #2
- Gold Metallic
- Unbleached Titanium (434)
- Mix #1
- Bronze Yellow (530)
- Permanent Light Blue (770)
- Mix #3
- Brilliant Blue (570)
- Phthalocyanine Blue (316)
- Burnt Sienna (127)
- Deep Brilliant Red (311)
- Cadmium Red Medium (154)
- Turquoise Green (560)
- Phthalocyanine Green (317)

2"

2 ½"

End View

MANGER
Top View

WOODEN NATIVITY SET

Scrap Fabric Crèche

The finished figurines are 3 inches to 6 inches tall.

MATERIALS

Scraps of wool, velveteen, cotton, felt, and brocade for the figurines
4½x7-inch piece *each* of brown solid fabric and wool fleece (or pile) for the sheep
4x8½-inch piece of burlap for the manger
One purchased crocheted doily for the baby
Scraps of ribbon, gold braid, rickrack, yarn, and other trims
Two white pipe cleaners
Twelve ¼-inch-diameter beads for figurines' hands
Assorted buttons and beads
Miniature containers for the wise men's gifts
Straw for the manger
Cardboard scraps for bases
Assorted embroidery floss for faces
Polyester fiberfill
Fabric glue
Tracing paper or plastic template material; pencil

INSTRUCTIONS

Patterns for the crèche figurines are *opposite* and on pages 56 and 57. Trace each pattern onto template plastic or tracing paper; cut out each plastic or paper template.

Making the wise men

The patterns for the faces, beards, and hoods are designed for machine appliqué, so no seam allowance is included. To appliqué by hand, add a scant ¼ inch seam allowance when cutting these pieces from fabric.

Cut each shape from the desired fabric.

Appliqué face pieces onto hoods; embroider faces and add crowns as desired. Appliqué hoods onto body pieces. Add trims to each body.

Fold each sleeve piece in half lengthwise with right sides together.

Stitch the raw edges of each sleeve together, leaving the angled shoulder edge open. Turn sleeves right out. Baste sleeves in place on body fronts, matching raw edges.

Stitch fronts and backs together, right sides together and leaving the bottoms open. Turn bodies right side out; stuff firmly with fiberfill.

Cut a cardboard base for each wise man. Cut a fabric circle ½ inch larger all around than the base. Hand-sew a fabric circle to the bottom of each body, slipping a cardboard base inside before closing the seam.

For hands, cover ¼-inch-diameter beads with scraps of face fabric. Sew hands in place at sleeve ends. Stitch or glue gift containers in place.

Making the baby

Appliqué the face piece onto the baby's hood; embroider face.

Baste the crocheted doily atop the body piece, matching top and side edges. Appliqué the hood onto the body, enclosing the edge of the doily.

Stitch front and back pieces together, right sides together and leaving an opening for turning. Turn right side out; hand-sew the opening closed.

Making the manger
Cut one manger piece from burlap. Fold the piece in half lengthwise with right sides together. Stitch the long edges together, leaving both ends open. Turn the tube right side out; insert stuffing.

Sew the ends of the manger together, making a doughnut shape. Spread straw along the edge of the manger; place the baby atop the straw with its head resting on the thickest part of the manger. Tack baby and straw to manger.

Making Mary, Joseph, shepherd
Using appropriate patterns and fabrics, make the remaining figurines in the same manner as the wise men. Use a scrap of fleece for the shepherd's collar. Bend a pipe cleaner into shape for the shepherd's crook; sew or glue it in the shepherd's hand.

Making the sheep
Cut two of the sheep pattern from brown fabric. Cut two more sheep bodies from the fleece, cutting away the face portion as indicated on the pattern, *left*. Baste the fleece onto the brown fabric, matching raw edges.

Stitch the two body pieces together, right sides together and leaving the bottom open. Clip curves and trim seam allowances as necessary; turn right side out.

Stuff the sheep body until firm, then hand-sew the opening closed. Embroider the sheep's face.

Cut two ears from scraps of the brown fabric. Tack the ears in place at the side of the sheep's head.

Cut a 2½-inch-long piece from the remaining pipe cleaner; bend it into a straight-sided U shape. Position the pipe cleaner under the body at the front and sew it in place for the front legs. Repeat to make the back legs.

Use a scrap of yarn or ravelled wool fabric to make the sheep's tail.

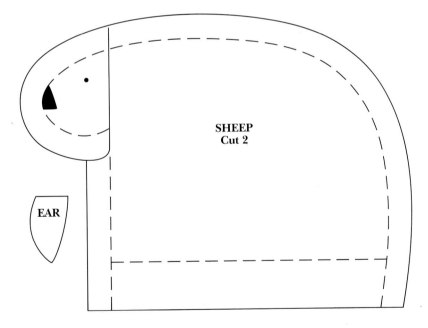

SHEEP
Cut 2

EAR

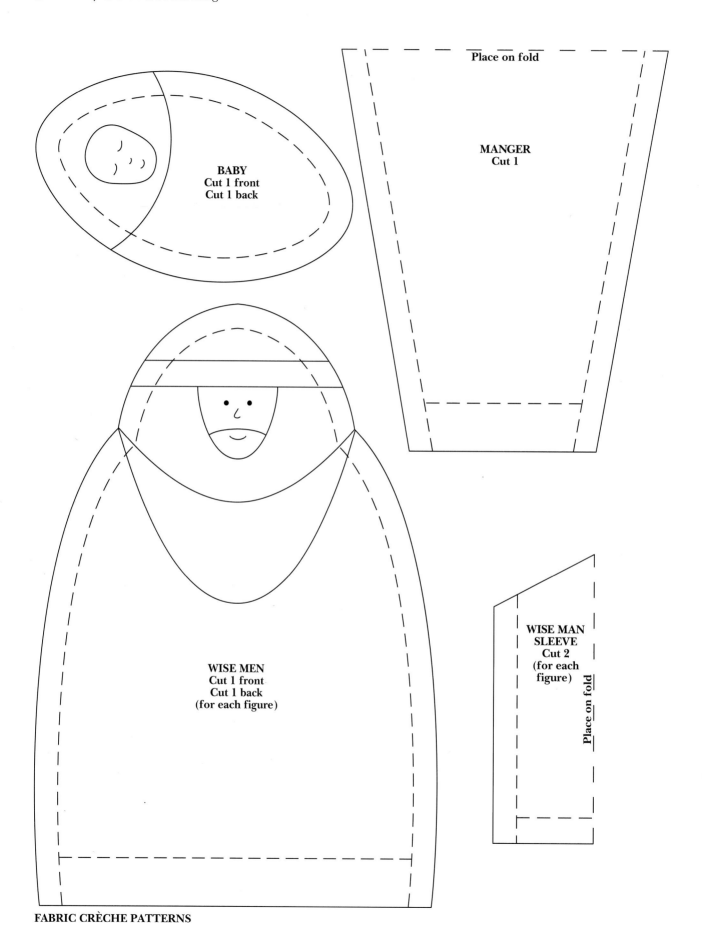

BABY
Cut 1 front
Cut 1 back

Place on fold

MANGER
Cut 1

WISE MEN
Cut 1 front
Cut 1 back
(for each figure)

**WISE MAN
SLEEVE**
Cut 2
(for each
figure)

Place on fold

FABRIC CRÈCHE PATTERNS

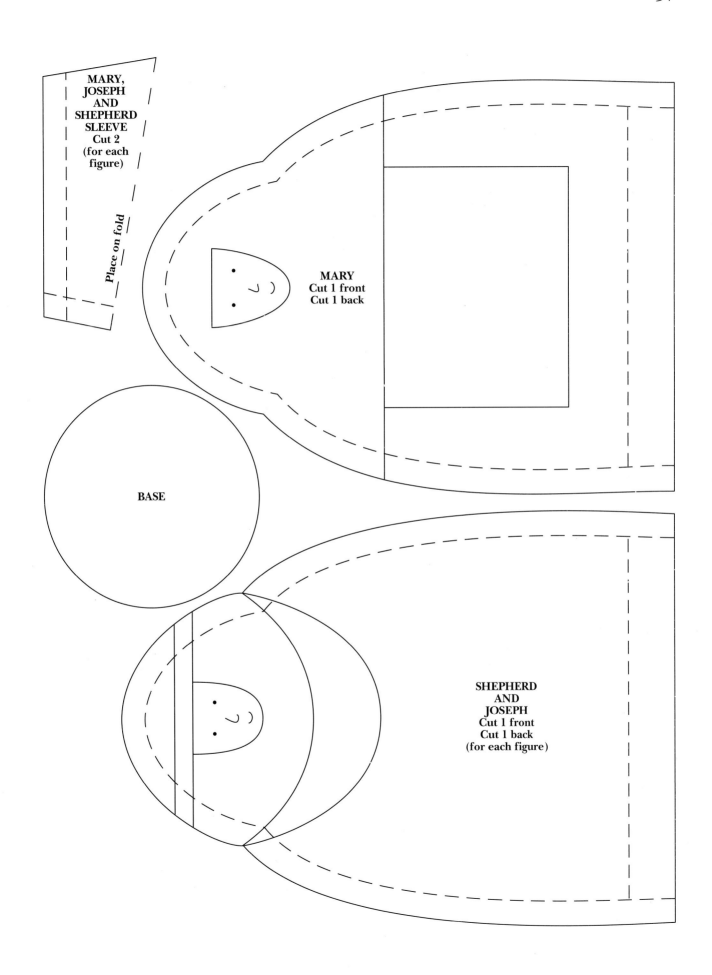

MARY,
JOSEPH
AND
SHEPHERD
SLEEVE
Cut 2
(for each
figure)

Place on fold

MARY
Cut 1 front
Cut 1 back

BASE

SHEPHERD
AND
JOSEPH
Cut 1 front
Cut 1 back
(for each figure)

Pinecone Nativity

The finished figurines are approximately 6 inches tall.

MATERIALS
For the figurines
Two 5½-inch-long pinecones and one 4½-inch-long pinecone

Flesh-colored oven-bake clay

Three 6x7-inch felt scraps for robes

Three 4x5½-inch rectangles of coordinating cotton fabrics for head coverings

Three 1-inch-diameter wooden beads for heads

Six $\frac{1}{16}$-inch-diameter black beads for eyes

Brown crepe-wool for hair

Scraps of perle cotton or embroidery floss for head ties

45 inches of jute twine for belts

One black or brown pipe cleaner for shepherd's crook

Scrap of gold poster board for halo

Black and red fine-tipped permanent markers for facial features

White crafts glue; hot-glue gun

Three ½-inch-thick wood circles (approximately 2¾ inches in diameter) or blocks for bases

For the baby and manger
4-inch square of white felt, fleece, or batting for the blanket

One 16 mm wooden bead for head

Large pinecone (2½ to 3 inches in diameter) for the manger

Excelsior or wood shavings for the manger

Red and white acrylic paints and paintbrush (optional)

For the two sheep
Two 1½- to 2-inch-diameter small, round pinecones for bodies

Two 1-inch-long oval pinecones for the heads

Two $\frac{1}{16}$-inch-diameter black beads for the eyes

Scraps of black felt for ears

Two white pipe cleaners for legs

Black and white acrylic paints

INSTRUCTIONS
Making the standing figurines
CLAY HEADS AND HANDS: Cover half of each 1-inch-diameter bead with a thin, flattened circle of clay.

Roll a ½-inch- to ¾-inch-long narrow tube of clay for each nose (make Mary's nose smaller than the others); push a tube into the center of each face. With your fingers, blend the top edge of the nose into the clay of the face, leaving the tip of the nose free.

For eyes, push two black beads into the clay of each face.

For hands, roll a ½-inch-diameter tube of clay 6 inches long. Cut the tube into six 1-inch-long segments. Round the ends slightly. Use a toothpick to make a hole through one hand for the shepherd's crook.

Following the manufacturer's directions, oven-bake the prepared clay pieces. Let the clay cool completely. Use fine-tipped markers to draw eyebrows and a mouth on Mary's face.

Remove some scales from one end of each pinecone, making a small indentation for the head. Hot-glue the heads in place.

ROBES: Cut a 4x7-inch rectangle of felt for each robe and two 2x2½-inch pieces for sleeves. If Mary's pinecone is smaller than the others, trim her robe to 3½x6½ inches.

Wrap a robe around each pinecone, overlapping the front edges at

an angle. Hot-glue the overlapped edges together. Tie 15 inches of jute or perle cotton around each waist.

Fold each sleeve in half lengthwise with right sides together. Stitch the long edges together, using a ¼-inch seam allowance. Turn each sleeve right side out and top-stitch across one end. Hot-glue a hand into the open end of each sleeve. Do not attach sleeves to robe yet.

HEAD COVERINGS: Press under a ½-inch-wide hem along one longer edge of each head-covering piece.

Apply white glue to the top and forehead of one figurine's head. Lay the folded edge of the head covering across the forehead.

Fold the sides of the head covering down along the sides of the figurine. Tightly wrap two 6-inch lengths of perle cotton around the head to hold the fabric; knot the threads together in the back. Dab glue on the forehead to hold the perle cotton in place.

Make head coverings for all the figurines in the same manner.

Glue the sleeves in place on each figurine, hiding the top of each sleeve under its head covering.

FINISHING TOUCHES: Cut ¾ inch of crepe for Joseph's beard. Pull the crepe to loosen the strands; then glue them in place around the sides and chin of the head. Glue a small strip of crepe under his nose for a moustache. Make the shepherd's beard in the same manner.

Glue a little piece of crepe under Mary's head covering for her hair. Cut a 1½-inch-diameter circle from the gold poster board; glue it to the back of her head.

Slip the pipe cleaner through the hole in the shepherd's hand. Bend the top over in the shape of a crook.

Glue the bottom of each pinecone onto a wood base.

Making the baby and manger
BABY: Mix red and white paints to get a pale pink. Paint the 16 mm wooden bead. Add spots of a darker pink for the cheeks. Use black marker to draw dots for eyes and mouth.

Cut one of the blanket pattern, *left*, from the white felt. Fold the tip of the

continued

Fold

Place on fold

BABY BLANKET

blanket down as indicated on the pattern; glue fold in place.

Spread white glue on the top and sides of the bead; place the bead atop the folded tip of the blanket. Fold the top of the blanket over the head and the angled sides around the head; let the glue dry. Fold the straight edges of the felt in toward the center. Glue the overlapped edges together.

Cut a ¾-inch-diameter circle of gold poster board; glue halo to back of baby's head.

MANGER: Cut a 1-inch slice off the tip of a 2½- to 3-inch-diameter pinecone. Remove the scales from the tip to make a small basin to hold the baby. Glue a small amount of excelsior around the indentation.

Spread glue on the back of the baby's blanket. Press baby into the manger and hold until the glue sets.

Making the sheep

Dab white acrylic paint over each pinecone; let paint dry. Glue a small oval cone onto the wider end of each round pinecone with the narrower end of the small cone becoming the sheep's nose. Glue black beads in place for eyes.

For the ears, cut teardrops of black felt approximately ¾ inch long. Glue ears in place on each head.

Cut each pipe cleaner in half. Dip both ends of each piece into black paint to make hooves. Bend each piece of pipe cleaner into a U shape.

Push pipe cleaner pieces between the scales of the body pinecone to position front and rear legs on each sheep; glue in place.

Pinecone Angel

Shown on page 59.
The finished angel is approximately 5 inches tall.

MATERIALS

One 5-inch-long pinecone
Flesh-colored oven-bake clay
5x10-inch scrap of white felt or fleece for the robe
3x10-inch rectangle of knit-backed gold lamé
1-inch-diameter wooden bead
Two 1/16-inch-diameter black beads for eyes
Brown crepe-wool for hair
12 inches of brass wire for halo
12 inches of gold thread or narrow cord for the hanger
Two 22 mm star-shaped imitation jewels; gold spray paint
One 2½-inch-long round toothpick
Scrap of polyester fiberfill
Red acrylic paint and paintbrush
Black and red fine-tipped permanent markers for facial features
White crafts glue; hot-glue gun
Purchased star-shaped confetti
Tracing paper and pencil

INSTRUCTIONS

HEAD AND HANDS: Make a head and two hands from clay in the same manner as described for the nativity figurines on page 58. Before baking the clay, use a toothpick to make a hole in one hand for the wand.

After baking the face, paint rosy cheeks on the face with diluted red acrylic paint. Use the red marker to draw a small heart for the mouth. With the black marker, add eyebrows, lashes, and a curved smile through the heart mouth.

Glue head to top of the pinecone. Cut a 1½-inch length of crepe for the hair. Gently loosen the strands, then glue the hair in place on the head.

Form the brass wire into a 1-inch-diameter circle; twist the ends of the wire together. Glue the halo to the pinecone at the back of the head.

ROBE: Cut a 4½x7-inch rectangle of felt for the angel's robe. Fold over a ½-inch hem on one long edge of the rectangle. With the hem to the outside, wrap the felt around the pinecone; overlap the edges at an angle at the center front. Tack or glue the edges in place.

From the remaining felt, cut two 2x2½-inch pieces for sleeves. Follow the instructions for making robes on page 58 to stitch and turn the two sleeves. Glue the sleeves in place under the collar of the angel's robe and add the hands.

WINGS: Trace the wings pattern, *left*.

With right sides together, fold the lamé into a 3x5-inch rectangle. Trace the outline of the wings pattern onto the wrong side of the fabric.

Machine-stitch on the drawn line, leaving an opening for turning as indicated on the pattern. Cut out the sewn piece from the fabric, leaving a ¼-inch seam allowance. Clip curves, then turn the wings right side out. Stuff the wings lightly; hand-sew the opening closed.

Tack the wings in place at the center back of the angel.

FINISHING TOUCHES: Use gold spray paint to paint the toothpick for the wand; let paint dry. Push the toothpick into the hole in the angel's hand. Hot-glue a star-shaped jewel to the end of the toothpick.

Glue the remaining star-shaped jewel to the front of the angel's robe. Glue star confetti on robe as desired.

Stitch the gold thread through the collar at the center back; tie the ends of the thread together to make a hanging loop.

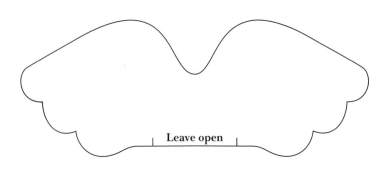

Leave open

Treasured Keepsakes
TO MAKE AHEAD

For many families, the holidays aren't quite right without that one cherished decoration, passed down from generations before. Whether it's a stocking or a picture, an afghan, or a particular ornament, family tradition gives it special meaning and memories.

Create your own legacy with any of these lovely holiday decorations. Start early, making a gift of love that will become a treasured keepsake. Even at the last minute, you'll find in this book quick and easy things to make that are the fuel of future memory at the heart of our Christmas homes.

Plaid Throw With Cross-Stitched Ornament Garland

Throw measures 45x58 inches. Garland stitch count is 53 high and 123 wide.

MATERIALS

1⅜ yards of 60-inch-wide plaid wool flannel

Two 1¾x47-inch strips of blue solid wool flannel

14x51-inch piece of 18-count ivory Heartsong or Aida cloth

Two 8¾x24-inch pieces of lightweight ivory lining fabric

One skein *each* of embroidery floss in colors listed in color key, *opposite*, except when additional skeins are indicated in parentheses

Clear acrylic sewing thread

INSTRUCTIONS

For cross-stitch, use six strands of floss over two threads of Heartsong or Aida fabric except when the key indicates the use of blended threads. Begin by stitching one ornament garland centered on the fabric, omitting *both* end sections indicated by the vertical lines on the chart.

Stitch a second garland to the right of the center motif, omitting the left end section. Stitch a third garland to the left of the center motif, omitting the end section at the right.

When stitching is complete, trim 2 inches from each short edge of the design fabric. Trim the top edge to 1⅜ inches above the stitching and the bottom edge 1⅝ inches below the stitching. Machine-sew a loose zigzag stitch around all edges.

Join the two pieces of lining fabric to make one 8¾x47-inch strip. Press the seam allowances open.

Using a ⅜-inch seam allowance, baste the wrong side of the design fabric to the right side of the lining. Trim edges of lining close to basting.

Sew a strip of blue fabric to each long edge of the design unit, stitching directly over the basting. Press the seam allowances away from the design unit; baste the raw edge of the blue fabric in place on the back.

Trim plaid fabric to 47x60 inches; stay-stitch all edges. Position the design unit 7 inches from the bottom edge of the plaid fabric. Using clear thread, topstitch in the seam line between the design fabric and the blue trim, stitching through all layers.

Press under a 1-inch hem on all edges; topstitch, using clear thread.

COLOR KEY

Anchor		DMC	
002	·	000	white
047	✗	304	christmas red - med
011	✱	350	coral - med dk
267	#	470	avocado green - med lt (4)
266	H	471	avocado green - lt (2)
306	◇	725	topaz - med (1)
386	◊	746	off white
307	◫	783	christmas gold
133	■	796	royal blue - dk
043	▶	815	garnet - med dk
187	◡	992	aquamarine - dk
886	≋	3047	yellow beige - lt
268	●	3345	hunter green - dk (2)

Blended needle:

727 (4 strands) & 091 star yellow KREINIK BALGER® blending filament (3 strands)	○
817 (4 strands) & 003HL red KREINIK BALGER® blending filament (3 strands)	✱
382	352 (4 strands) & 021 copper KREINIK BALGER® blending filament (3 strands)	□
011	964 (4 strands) & 094 star blue KREINIK BALGER® blending filament (3 strands)	+

798 (4 strands) & 032 pearl KREINIK BALGER® blending filament (3 strands)	◇
907 (4 strands) & 015 char-treuse KREINIK BALGER® blending filament (3 strands)	∩
746 (4 strands) & 032 pearl KREINIK BALGER® blending filament (3 strands)	J
000 (4 strands) & 032 pearl KREINIK BALGER® blending filament (3 strands)	△

002	000	right side of striped ornament (2 strands)
133	796	decoration on blue ornament (2 strands)
019	817	decoration on blue ornament (2 strands)
		003HL red KREINIK BALGER® blending filament—decoration on gold ornament (3 strands)
307	783	beads (2 strands)
212	561	leaves under dove (2 strands)

Straight stitch:

| 212 | 561 | branches (2 strands) |

Backstitch:

| 382 | 3371 | left sides of pine cone & round, striped ornaments (2 strands) |
| 011 | 350 | right side of pine cone ornament (2 strands) |

Fabrics and finished design sizes:

11 Aida, 4-7/8"h x 11-1/4"w
14 Aida, 3-7/8"h x 8-7/8"w
18 Aida, 3"h x 6-7/8"w
22 Hardanger, 2-1/2"h x 5-5/8"w

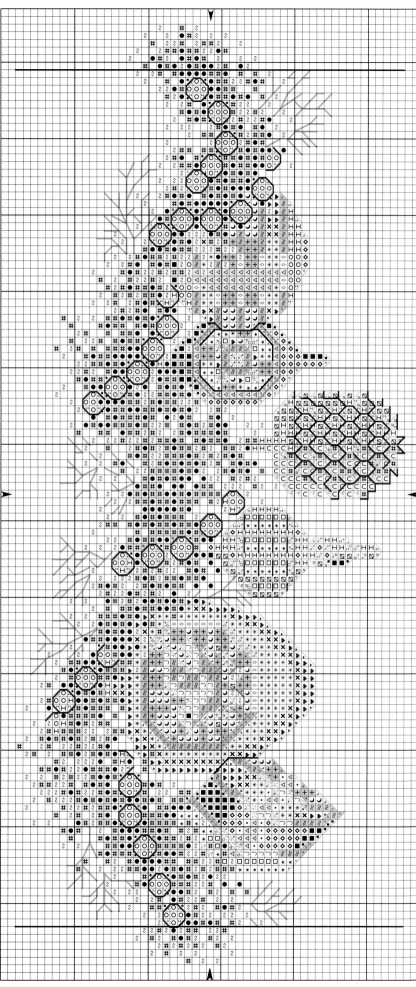

PLAID THROW WITH CROSS-STITCHED ORNAMENT GARLAND

1 Square = 1 Stitch

Victorian Knitted Stockings

Stockings are 18½ inches long.

MATERIALS

For the woman's stocking

One 50-gram ball *each* of Lane Borgosesia Hilton yarn in wine (No. 1161), pink (No. 1151), and white (No. 2428)

Paternayan Persian 3-strand yarn (1-yard lengths) in the following amounts and colors: 8 lengths of blue (No. 582); 5 lengths *each* of dark rose (No. 903) and light rose (No. 905); 4 lengths *each* of rose (No. 904), dark green (No. 575), and green (No. 574)

1½ yards of ⅛-inch-wide light turquoise satin ribbon

1 yard of ¹⁄₁₆-inch-wide wine ribbon

1 yard *each* of ⅛-inch-wide satin ribbon in the following colors: wine, medium rose, light rose, and dark green

One package *each* of 3 mm dark pink pearls and 4 to 6 mm pink glass beads

12 purchased small ribbon roses in shades of pink and wine

For the man's stocking

One 50-gram ball *each* of Lane Borgosesia Hilton yarn in dark green (No. 3346), white (No. 2428), and wine (No. 1161)

Paternayan Persian 3-strand yarn (1-yard lengths) in the following colors and amounts: 7 lengths *each* of dark green (No. 575), dark gold (No. 700) and green (No. 574); 4 lengths *each* of red (No. 942) and gold (No. 711); 3 lengths of light gold (No. 712)

2 yards of ⅛-inch-wide wine satin ribbon

1 yard of ⅛-inch-wide red satin ribbon

1½ yards of ¹⁄₁₆-inch-wide dark green satin ribbon

½ yard *each* of ⅛-inch-wide light green and light yellow satin ribbon and ¹⁄₁₆-inch-wide medium yellow satin ribbon

One package *each* of 6 mm ecru and 8 mm red glass beads

For both stockings

Size 1 knitting needles

Size 4 circular knitting needle (11½ inches long)

Size 4 double-pointed knitting needles (dpn); stitch marker

Scissors; ruler

Matching sewing threads

Sewing needle and tapestry needle

Abbreviations: See page 67.
Gauge: 6 sts and 8 rows = 1x1 inch in st st.

INSTRUCTIONS

For the woman's stocking

With wine yarn and circular Size 4 needle, cast on 72 sts. Place marker and join, taking care not to twist sts.

Rnds 1, 3, and 5: P.

Rnds 2 and 4: K.

Rnd 6: * K 5 wine, k 1 white, rep from * around.

Rnd 7: K 1 white, * k 3 wine, k 3 white, rep from * around; end k 2 white.

Rnd 8: K 2 white, * k 1 wine, k 5 white, rep from * around; end k 3 white; fasten off wine.

Rnds 9–20: K with white.

Rnd 21: Rep Rnd 8.

Rnd 22: Rep Rnd 7.

Rnd 23: Rep Rnd 6; fasten off.

Rnds 24, 26, 28, and 30: K with wine.

Rnds 25, 27, and 29: P with wine.

Continue with wine in st st (k every rnd) until piece measures 6½ inches from cast-on.

**Dec rnd:* K 1, k 2 tog, k around to last 3 sts, sl 1, k 1, psso, k 1—70 sts. K 7 rnds even. Rep from ** 5 times more; work 4 rnds even after last dec rnd—60 sts.

SETTING UP THE HEEL: *Note:* These instructions make a place for the heel, which is inserted later.

With wine, k 30, drop wine; with a piece of contrasting yarn, k 15, sl

KITCHENER STITCH

marker, k 15, sl the 30 waste sts back onto the left needle, drop waste yarn and k same 30 sts with wine. K even with wine until stocking measures 16 inches from cast-on; fasten off wine.

TOE: *Rnd 1:* Change to dpn and set up needles as follows: Join pink and k 15 sts with the first needle; k 30 with the second needle; k 15 with the third needle; place marker for beg of rnd between first and third needle.

Rnd 2: K to last 3 sts on needle, k 2 tog, k 1; on second needle sl 1, k 1, psso, k to last 3 sts, k 2 tog, k 1; on third needle, sl 1, k 1, psso, k to end.

Rnd 3: K even.

Rep rnds 2 and 3 until first and third needles contain 4 sts each, and the second needle contains 8 sts—16 sts. Fasten off leaving a 15-inch tail. Using a tapestry needle, graft sts from first and second needles to the sts on the third needle with the Kitchener stitch. Weave in ends.

HEEL: Carefully remove waste yarn. Divide and sl 30 lps above heel opening to first and second needle; pick up one extra lp (twist st to prevent holes) at the outside ends of each needle to close corner gaps—16 sts on each needle. Sl 30 lps below heel opening to third needle; pick up one extra lp at each end of needle to close corner gaps—32 sts. Join pink yarn at beg of first needle.

Rnd 1: K even.

Rnd 2: Rep Rnd 2 as for Toe.

Rnd 3: K even.

Rep rnds 2 and 3 until 6 sts rem on first and second needles, and 12 sts rem on third needle. Fasten off leaving a 15-inch tail. Using a tapestry needle, graft sts from first and third needles to the sts on the second needle with the Kitchener stitch. Weave in ends; block lightly.

HANGING LOOP: Using the Size 1 needles and wine yarn, pick up 5 sts along cast-on edge at beg of rnd (center back). K 40 rows; bind off. Sew the bound-off edge to the last garter st ridge (Rnd 5 of stocking).

continued

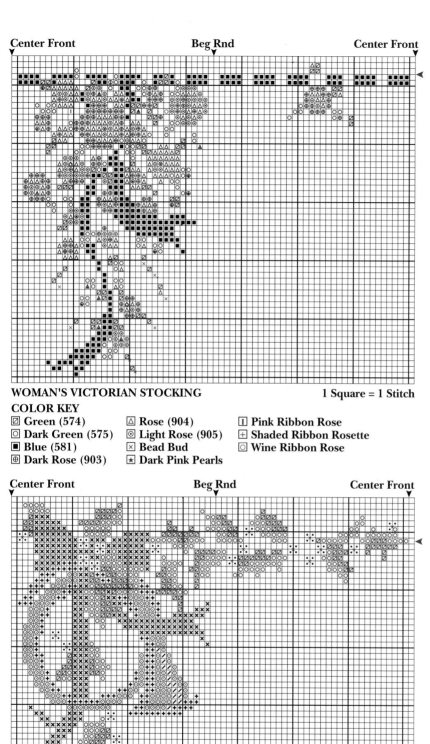

Center Front   **Beg Rnd**   **Center Front**

WOMAN'S VICTORIAN STOCKING   **1 Square = 1 Stitch**
COLOR KEY

☑ **Green (574)**	△ **Rose (904)**	⊞ **Pink Ribbon Rose**
◎ **Dark Green (575)**	◉ **Light Rose (905)**	⊞ **Shaded Ribbon Rosette**
■ **Blue (581)**	✕ **Bead Bud**	◎ **Wine Ribbon Rose**
⊕ **Dark Rose (903)**	✱ **Dark Pink Pearls**	

Center Front   **Beg Rnd**   **Center Front**

MAN'S VICTORIAN STOCKING   **1 Square = 1 Stitch**
COLOR KEY

☑ **Green (574)**	⊞ **Dark Gold (700)**	☑ **Light Gold (712)**	☒ **Wine Yarn**
◎ **Dark Green (575)**	◎ **Gold (711)**	• **Red (942)**	☒ **Red Bead**

DUPLICATE STITCH: Separate the Persian yarn; use one strand to work duplicate stitches (see stitch diagram, *below*). The red arrow on the chart, *left*, indicates the starting position. Stitch flower and ribbon design on stocking, centering according to the chart. Beg stitching design five rows beneath the last rnd of garter st. Backstitch or duplicate-stitch name on front of white panel at top of stocking. When stitching is done, block design area. Sew ribbon roses, dark pink pearls, and bead buds in place as indicated on the chart.

TASSEL: Cut 16-inch lengths of the assorted ribbons and 15-inch lengths of the single-strand Persian yarns and knitting yarns. Place a pink glass bead on the end of each ribbon; tie a knot at each end to keep beads on ribbon. Gather all strands into a bundle.

Tie the bundle in the center with three strands of blue Persian yarn; do not cut ends. Fold bundle in half at tie. Wrap a 1-yard strand of wine yarn 20 times tightly around the folded bundle 1 inch from the blue knot. Use the tapestry needle to pull wine yarn ends into the tassel's center. Thread the ends of the blue yarn into the needle; pull ends through stocking at the base of the hanging loop. Knot ends securely inside stocking.

For the man's stocking
Follow instructions on page 64 for the woman's stocking, except for the directions below. Use dark green instead of wine and white for the toe and heel.

Rnds 1–5: Follow instructions for woman's stocking.

Rnd 6: K 2 dark green, * k 3 white, k 3 dark green, rep from * around; end k 1 dark green.

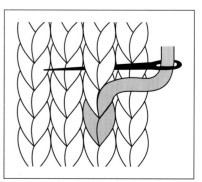

DUPLICATE STITCH

Rnd 7: * K 1 dark green, k 5 white, rep from * around.

Rnd 8: Rep Rnd 7.

Rnds 9–20: K even in white.

Rnds 21 and 22: Rep Rnd 7.

Rnd 23: Rep Rnd 6; fasten off.

Rnds 24 to end: Work as for woman's stocking, substituting dark green for wine and white for pink. Make the hanger loop in dark green.

Duplicate-stitch the design following the chart *opposite, bottom,* and beginning at the center front of the stocking in the eighth row beneath the last garter st row. The arrow on chart indicates the starting position.

When all stitching is complete, sew red beads over red stitches for berries. Make the tassel in the same manner as for the woman's stocking, except use the colors indicated in the materials list. Attach ecru glass beads to both ends of each ribbon.

Peace, Love, and Joy Greeting Card Holder

Greeting card holder measures approximately 8x18 inches, not including hanging loops. The stitch count for each heart motif is 51 high and 53 wide.

MATERIALS

8½x20-inch piece of 14-count Aida cloth

Embroidery floss in colors listed in color key on page 68

½ yard of red print fabric

¼ yard of white lining fabric

8¾x18-inch piece *each* of fusible interfacing and polyester fleece

⅜ yard *each* of ⅛- and ⅜-inch-wide red grosgrain ribbon

⅝ yard *each* of ¼- and 1-inch-wide red grosgrain ribbon

22½-inch-long dowel with finials

Four 22 mm gold jingle bells

Figure 1

Figure 1

INSTRUCTIONS

Use sewing thread to baste lines on Aida, dividing it into thirds as shown in Figure 1, *above.* Center and stitch one heart motif from pages 68 and 69 in each rectangle, using three strands of floss for cross-stitches. Use one strand for backstitches unless more strands are indicated on the key. When stitching is complete, trim 1 inch from all sides of the Aida.

Following manufacturer's instructions, fuse interfacing to back of Aida. Cut a piece of white lining fabric to match the Aida. Using a ¼-inch seam allowance, baste lining to Aida with wrong sides together.

Cut the ⅜-inch-wide ribbon in half. Center one piece over each line of basting between stitched motifs; topstitch through all layers.

Cut a 1¾x18-inch strip of red fabric. Press one long edge under ⅜ inch. With right sides together and using a ⅜-inch seam allowance, sew the unpressed edge of the strip to the top edge of the Aida. Turn pressed edge of the red fabric over to the back of the unit; topstitch.

For the backing, cut two 8¾x18-inch pieces of red fabric, one matching piece of fleece, and four 5-inch lengths of 1-inch-wide ribbon. Fold each ribbon in half. Matching raw edges, baste ribbons to right side of one backing piece along one long edge as shown in Figure 2, *below.*

continued

Knitting and Crocheting Abbreviations

beg	begin(ning)
bet	between
CC	contrasting color
ch(s)	chain(s)
cont	continue
dc	double crochet
dec	decrease
grp	group
inc	increase
k	knit
LH	left-hand
lp(s)	loop(s)
lsc	long single crochet
MC	main color
p	purl
pat	pattern
psso	pass sl st over
rem	remain(ing)
rep	repeat
RH	right-hand
rnd	round
RS(F)	right side (facing)
sc	single crochet
sk	skip
sl	slip
sl st	slip stitch
sp	space
ssk	slip, slip, knit
st(s)	stitch(es)
st st	stockinette stitch
tbl	through back loop
tog	together
WS(F)	wrong side (facing)
yo	yarn over
*	repeat from * as indicated
**	repeat from ** as indicated
( )	repeat between ( ) as indicated
[ ]	repeat between [ ] as indicated

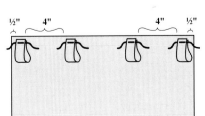

Figure 2

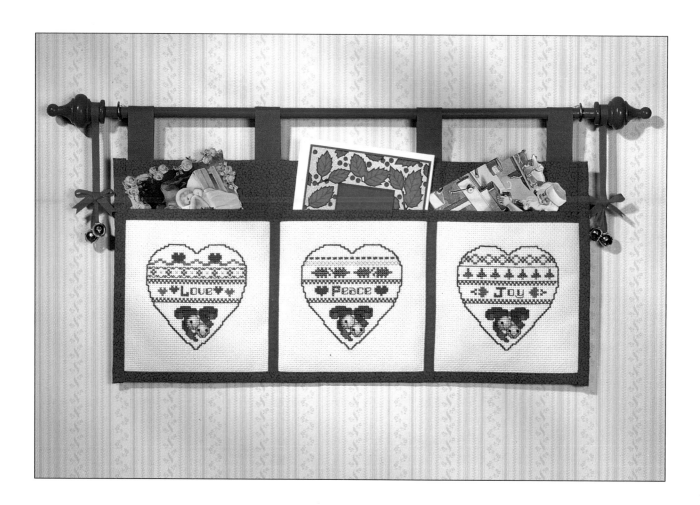

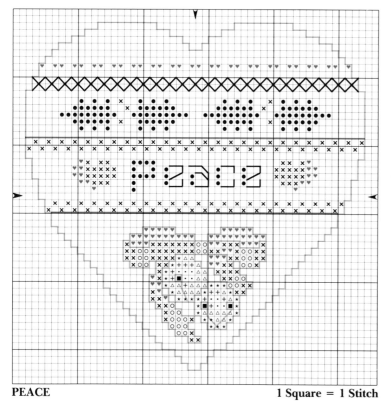

COLOR KEY

Anchor		DMC	
047	✕ ✕	321	christmas red
267	● ●	469	avocado green - med
020	♥ ♥	498	christmas red - dk
306	△ △	725	topaz - med
301	+ +	744	yellow - lt
386	· ·	746	off white
307	★ ★	783	christmas gold
382	■ ■	3021	brown gray - vy dk
035	○ ○	3705	strawberry - dk

Backstitch:

020		498	heart outline (6 strands)
020		498	interior red lines, "Love", "Joy" (2 strands)
306		725	yellow band on Peace heart (2 strands)
267		469	green band on Love heart, "Peace" (2 strands)
382		3021	jingle bells & bows (1 strand)

Fabrics and finished design sizes:

11 Aida, 4-5/8"h x 4-3/4"w
14 Aida, 3-3/4"h x 3-3/4"w
18 Aida, 2-7/8"h x 2-7/8"w
22 Hardanger, 2-3/8"h x 2-3/8"w

PEACE   **1 Square = 1 Stitch**

Baste the fleece to the wrong side of the other piece of backing fabric.

With right sides together and using a ½-inch seam allowance, join backing pieces along top edge. Trim fleece from the seam allowance close to the stitching; turn and press. Baste remaining raw edges.

Baste design unit atop backing, aligning bottom and side edges. Topstitch between heart motifs through all layers and over previous ribbon stitching to create pockets.

From remaining red fabric, cut one 1¾x18-inch strip and two 1¾x9¼-inch strips. Press one long edge of each strip under ⅜ inch. Add the long strip to the bottom edge in the same manner as for the top of the design unit. Center and stitch short strips to sides, turning the extra fabric at each end to the back before topstitching.

Slide dowel through ribbon loops.

Wrap one end of a 5-inch-long piece of ¼-inch-wide ribbon around each finial; tack ribbon end to back of ribbon just below dowel.

Cut the ⅛-inch-wide ribbon into two 1½-inch-long and two 2-inch-long pieces. Thread a bell onto each piece. Tack the ends of one short and one long ribbon/bell unit to the end of each ribbon on the finials.

Cut the remaining ¼-inch-wide ribbon in half. Make two bows; tack bows over ends of ribbon/bell units.

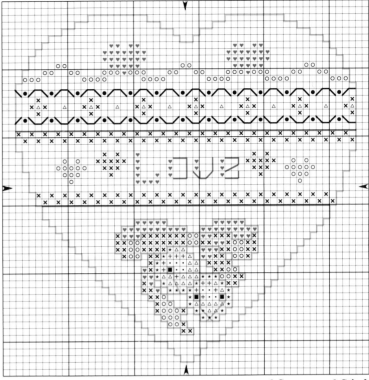

LOVE 1 Square = 1 Stitch

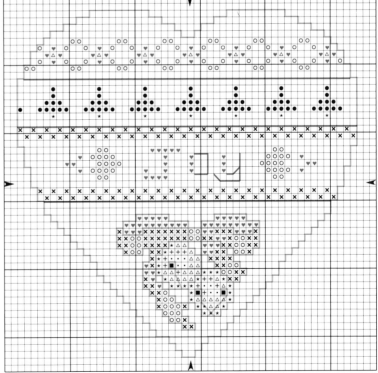

JOY 1 Square = 1 Stitch

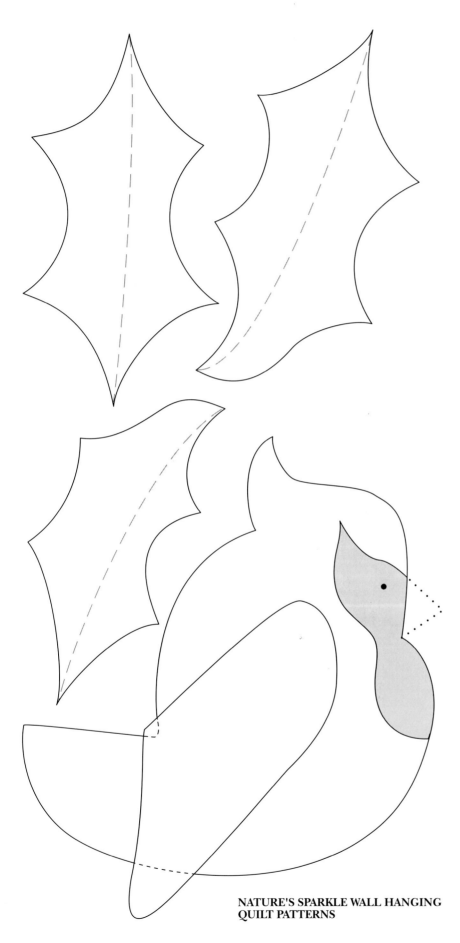

**NATURE'S SPARKLE WALL HANGING
QUILT PATTERNS**

Nature's Sparkle Wall Hanging Quilt

*The finished wall hanging measures
approximately 42 inches square.*

MATERIALS
1¼ yards of white-on-white or
   muslin for background fabric
¼ yard *each* of two dark red prints
½ yard *each* of five dark green print
   and solid fabrics
Ten 1-inch squares of light gold
   fabric for beaks
Scrap of black solid fabric for birds
1¼ yards of backing fabric
45-inch square of quilt batting
One 100-count package of 6 mm
   ruby beads for holly berries
One 100-count package of clear
   rocaille beads for snowflakes
10 small black beads for bird eyes
Template material; compass
Nonpermanent fabric marker
Fabric glue stick (optional)
Rotary cutter and acrylic ruler
Ecru and green quilting threads;
   quilting needle

INSTRUCTIONS
Cutting the fabrics
Cut a 2½x42-inch strip from each of
the red and green fabrics. Set these
aside for the binding.

   Make a template for the bird's
body, wing, mask, and each leaf from
the full-size patterns at *left*. Mark the
right side of each template. Draw
around each template on the *right*
side of the appropriate fabric, leaving
at least ½ inch between tracings.
When cutting, add a ¼-inch seam allowance around each piece.

   From *each* red fabric, cut five bird
bodies and wings. Cut half of the
birds with the templates faceup and
half with templates facedown. From
the black fabric, cut five birds' masks
with the template faceup and five
more with the template facedown.

   With templates faceup, cut seven
of each leaf from *each* green fabric.
Repeat with the templates facedown.

   Save the remainder of the red and
green fabrics for the binding.

   Cut one 42½-inch square of background fabric. Use a fabric marker to
draw 18-inch-diameter and 32-inch-

diameter circles in the center of the fabric. Use these marked circles as guidelines for positioning the wreath.

Positioning the appliqué
Aligning outside edges, position a mask on each bird body. On each mask, turn under the seam allowance on all interior edges and appliqué them in place on the red fabric.

Turn under and baste the seam allowances on all the remaining pieces.

Referring to the photo, *above,* pin the 10 birds evenly spaced around the wreath. Pin wings atop bodies.

Arrange five leaves in each corner of the background square as shown, placing them at least 1½ inches from the edges of the fabric. Hold leaves in place with pins or with fabric glue.

Fill in the wreath with leaves, letting some extend over the circle guidelines and overlapping some for variety of placement. Mix fabrics and leaf shapes randomly.

Making the bird beaks
Fold each gold square in half diagonally to form a triangle. Fold the tri-

FIGURE 1

angle corners in so the fabric edges meet in the center of a square as illustrated in Figure 1, *above.* Baste the raw edges to hold them in place.

continued

Appliquéing the birds and wreath

Appliqué all pieces in place, working on one section of the quilt at a time. As you appliqué each bird, slip a beak under the mask; leave the outside edges of the beak unstitched.

Quilting and finishing

Mark the quilting design before adding backing and batting.

The quilting in the center of the wreath is made by repeating and overlapping holly leaves, similar to the manner in which the appliqués were laid out. Using a nonpermanent fabric marker, trace the leaf templates to mark a quilting design.

Mark the background outside the wreath with freehand swirls and squiggles, filling in empty spaces with random holly leaves and hearts.

Cut 43-inch squares of batting and backing fabric. Sandwich the batting between the quilt top and backing. Baste all layers securely together.

Quilt the background with ecru thread. After each group of approximately 10 stitches, slide a clear bead down the thread onto the quilt top to create the sparkle of fresh snow.

Use green thread to quilt a vein down the center of each holly leaf.

Sewing through all layers, give each bird a black bead eye. Add ruby beads where you want holly berries. If you have clear beads remaining, use them to fill in wherever you like—on the background, on a leaf, or even on a bird.

To make binding, sew together the remaining strips of red and green fabrics into a rectangle; press seams open. From this patchwork, cut bias strips 2½ inches wide. Seam all the bias strips end to end to make continuous binding about 170 inches long.

With wrong sides together, press the binding strip in half lengthwise; handle the fabric carefully to avoid stretching the bias edges.

Beginning in the center of any quilt side and taking a ¼-inch seam allowance, sew the raw edge of the binding to the edge of the quilt. Miter corners. Overlap 1 inch of binding at the starting point.

Trim batting and backing. Turn the folded edge of the binding over the seam allowance to the back of the quilt; hand-stitch binding to backing.

Papier-Mâché Bell Ornament

The bell ornament is 3 inches tall.

MATERIALS
1-pound package of instant papier-mâché powdered mix (we used Celluclay Instant Papier-Mâché)
Mixing bowl or large plastic bag
Three 3-inch-tall plastic foam bells
¾ yard of ¼-inch-wide red ribbon
19-gauge wire
Leather tool for modeling
Packaged 10 mm red wooden beads
Acrylic paint in ecru, red, and dark green; small paintbrush
Hot-glue gun; white crafts glue
Clear acrylic spray sealer
Wire cutters; needle-nosed pliers

INSTRUCTIONS
This bell ornament can hang on a tree or can be used to make other holiday decorations as shown. Add a sprig of mistletoe, if you like.

Mixing the papier-mâché
Pour one-fourth of the papier-mâché powder into a mixing bowl or large plastic bag (the bag will hold in the dust that rises from the powder). Following the manufacturer's directions, add water and knead the mixture to obtain a claylike consistency. Note the package directions for proper storage of powder and unused portions of the prepared clay.

Applying the papier-mâché clay
Firmly press a marble-size ball of clay onto a bell form. Dip your hands in warm water, then use your wet fingers to smooth the clay in a thin layer over the surface of the bell. Continue adding clay in this manner until each bell is completely covered.

Cut three 1-inch pieces of wire; bend each piece into a U shape. While the clay is still wet, push the ends of one wire loop into the center top of each bell, leaving enough exposed loop for a piece of ribbon or wire to pass through for a hanger. Set the bells aside to dry.

Using your hands and the modeling tool, shape six or more holly leaves out of clay. Use a small piece of wire to make holes in the leaves where they will be wired to the bells later.

Let the clay dry one to three days before painting.

Painting the bells and leaves
When leaves and bells are completely dry, cover each shape with a coating of thinned crafts glue; let dry. Paint the leaves green. Paint the bells ecru; let dry. Decorate the bells as desired (we painted green teardrops, red hearts, and dots).

When paint is dry, spray each shape with acrylic sealer; let dry.

Adding the wire extensions
Cut six 5-inch-long pieces of wire. Wrap each piece loosely around the paintbrush handle or the shaft of a pencil, then slide it off gently to retain the coiled shape.

Put a dab of glue on one end of the wire coil; carefully push the glued end of the coil into the center bottom of each bell, pushing it through the hardened clay and into the foam bell. Hold the wire in place; let the glue dry. Thread a bead onto the bottom of each wire; bend wire end to hold bead in place.

Use pliers to wrap one end of another wire coil around the loop at the top of each bell. Use pliers to bend the sharp end of the wire safely out of harm's way. Glue leaves and beads onto the free ends of each coil.

Hanging the bells
Cut an 8-inch-long piece of red ribbon. Fold the ribbon in half and push both ends through the loop at the top of one bell. Knot the ribbon ends in the back of the bell to hold the hanging loop in place. Use the remaining ribbon to make a bow. Tie or glue the bow in place atop the bell, covering the ribbon knot. Hang the bell on a tree or from a hook.

Instead of ribbon, we used wire coils to hang some of our bells. By making hangers different lengths, we created the look of a mobile simply by hanging three bells side by side.

Cross-Stitched Cranberries Trivets ·

The trivets are approximately 5¼ inches square and 8½ inches square. Stitch count for the small trivet is 62 square. The large trivet is 98-square stitches.

MATERIALS

For the small trivet

8-inch square *each* of ivory taffeta and 14-count Damask Aida fabric

Embroidery floss in colors listed in color key, *opposite*

Two 6-inch squares of heavy fleece

For the large trivet

11-inch square *each* of ivory taffeta and 14-count Damask Aida fabric

Embroidery floss in colors listed in color key, *opposite*

Two 9-inch squares of heavy fleece

INSTRUCTIONS

Using three strands of floss, center and stitch the appropriate cranberry motif on the Aida fabric. Use one strand of floss for backstitches.

When stitching is complete, trim Aida 1 inch beyond the design on all sides. Cut taffeta and fleece to the same size.

Place Aida and taffeta with right sides together; lay fleece atop the Aida. Using a ½-inch seam allowance, stitch around the square, leaving a 2-inch opening in one side for turning. Clip corners; turn right side out. Slip-stitch opening closed.

CROSS-STITCHED CRANBERRIES TRIVET

1 Square = 1 Stitch

COLOR KEY

Anchor		DMC	
002	`· ·`	000	white
216	`I I`	320	pistachio green - med lt
047	`# #`	321	christmas red
216	`Ø Ø`	367	pistachio green - med
335	`O O`	606	orange red - bright
868	`✶ ✶`	758	terra cotta - lt
264	`∿ ∿`	772	leaf green - lt
043	`● ●`	815	garnet - med dk
380	`▲ ▲`	838	beige brown - vy dk

378	`∩ ∩`	841	beige brown - lt
072	`♥ ♥`	902	garnet - vy dk
347	`◊ ◊`	945	pink beige

Backstitch:

072		902	berries (1 strand)
5968		355	flowers (1 strand)
879		890	leaves (1 strand)
380		838	all other backstitching (1 strand)

Straight stitch:

5968		355	tips of flowers (1 strand)

Fabrics and finished design sizes:

11 Aida, 9-3/8"h x 9"w
14 Aida, 7-3/8"h x 7"w
18 Aida, 5-3/4"h x 5-1/2"w
22 Hardanger, 4-3/4"h x 4-1/2"w

Log Cabin Afghan And Pillow

The afghan measures 41x55 inches. The pillow top is 12 inches square.

MATERIALS
For the afghan

Coats and Clark's Red Heart Classic yarn (3.5-ounce skeins) in the following amounts and colors: five skeins of red (No. 914); two skeins *each* of emerald (No. 676), green (No. 675), and bright blue (No. 822); and one skein *each* of peacock (No. 508), parakeet (No. 513), and forest green (No. 689)

Size F/5 crochet hook

Large-eyed yarn needle

For the coordinating pillow

One additional skein *each* of blue, parakeet, and green yarn

14-inch square *each* of pillow lining and backing fabrics; additional fabric for a ruffle or other desired finish

Polyester filling

Abbreviations: See page 67.

Gauge: Each Log Cabin square is 7 inches square.

INSTRUCTIONS
Making the Log Cabin square

Make 35 Log Cabin squares for the afghan and one square for the pillow.

CENTER SQUARE: With red, ch 12.

Row 1: RSF, sc in second ch from hook; * ch 1, sk ch, sc in next ch. * Repeat from * to * across. Ch 1, turn.

Row 2: Sc in first sc, * ch 1, sk ch, sc in next sc. * Repeat from * to * across. Ch 1, turn.

Rows 3–10: Rep Row 2. Fasten off.

LOGS 1 AND 2: Work across top of red square for Log 1 and bottom of square for Log 2.

Row 1: With peacock, draw up a lp in end sc of center square; ch 1. RSF, sc in each sc and ch-1 sp across (11 scs). Ch 1, turn.

Row 2: WSF, sc in first sc, * ch 1, sk 1 sc, sc in next sc.* Repeat from * to * across. Ch 1, turn.

Row 3: RSF, rep Row 2 of center square. Fasten off.

LOGS 3 AND 4: Work across each side, across peacock log, the center square, and next peacock log.

Row 1: With parakeet yarn, draw up a lp in side of end sc of peacock log; ch 1. With RSF, sc in each st, including ch, across the side (17 scs). Ch 1, turn.

Rows 2 and 3: Repeat Rows 2 and 3 of Log 1. Fasten off.

LOGS 5 AND 6: Work across top and bottom.

Row 1: With forest green, draw up a lp in side of end sc of parakeet log; ch 1. With RSF, sc in each sc and ch-1 sp across. Ch 1, turn.

Rows 2 and 3: Repeat Rows 2 and 3 of Log 1. Fasten off.

LOGS 7–12: With green yarn, work logs 7 and 8 across each side; rep logs 5 and 6 (23 scs). Work logs 9 and 10 with emerald yarn across top and bottom; rep logs 5 and 6 (23 scs). Work logs 11 and 12 across sides with blue yarn; rep logs 5 and 6 (29 scs). Fasten off, leaving 15-inch-long tails of yarn for sewing.

Weave in yarn ends on the back side of each square. Sew ends down with matching thread, if desired.

Assembling the afghan squares

Arrange the squares in seven horizontal rows of five squares each, turning the squares to alternate blue and green edges. Use the yarn tails to whip the squares together, sewing through the front lps of each st. Weave in tails not needed for sewing.

Adding the afghan border

With red yarn, draw up a lp in any sc on the outside edge; ch 1.

Rnd 1: With RSF, sc in each st around edge. Work sc in each sc, ch-1 sp, and edge of sc row; work sc in each joining seam between rows. In each corner sc, (sc, ch 2, sc). Join last sc to first. Ch 3.

Rnd 2: With RSF, dc in each sc around, working (dc, ch 2, dc) in each ch-2 sp at corners. Join last dc to top of beg ch 3. Ch 1.

Rnd 3: Sc in each dc around, working (sc, ch 2, sc) in each corner ch-2 sp. Join last sc to first. Fasten off.

Rnd 4: With red yarn, beg in second sc from corner on one short side;

ch 1. Sc in first sc, * sk 1 sc, (**2 dcs, ch 2, 2 dcs—shell made**) in corner ch-2 sp, sk 1 sc, sc in next sc. ** Sk 2 scs, shell in next sc, sk 2 scs, sc in next sc. Rep from ** across to next corner, then rep from * to **. At end of rnd, join last dc of shell to beg sc; turn. Sl st to ch-2 sp of next shell; ch 1, turn.

Rnd 5: With WSF, * sc in ch-2 sp of shell, work shell in next sc. * Rep from * to * around. At corners, work sc in second dc of corner shell, shell in corner ch-2 sp, sc in next dc of shell. At end of rnd, join last dc of shell to beg sc; turn. Sl st to ch-2 sp of next shell; ch 1, turn.

Rnd 6: With RSF, rep Rnd 5. Join as before. Ch 3, turn.

Rnd 7: With WSF, * shell in ch-2 sp of next shell, dc in next sc. * Rep from * to * around, working (3 dcs, ch 2, 3 dcs) in each corner ch-2 sp. At end of rnd, join last dc of shell to top of beg ch 3. Ch 1, turn.

Rnd 8: With RSF, sc in next dc and in each dc around, working (sc, ch 2, sc) in each corner ch-2 sp. Join last sc to first. Sl st to next ch-2 sp.

Rnd 9: Ch 3, sl st in same ch-2 sp. Ch 2, sk 3 scs. Work corner pattern: (sl st, ch 3, sl st) in next sc, ch 3, sk 4 scs, (sl st, ch 3, sl st, ch 5, sl st, ch 3, sl st) in ch-2 sp of corner. Ch 3, sk 4 scs, (sl st, ch 3, sl st) in next sc. * Ch 2, sk 3 scs, (sl st, ch 3, sl st) in ch-2 sp, ch 2, sk 3 scs, sl st in next sc. * Repeat from * to * around, working corner pattern at each corner. At end of rnd, sl st in beg ch-2 sp. Fasten off.

Weave in yarn ends on back side. Block afghan as needed.

Making the coordinating pillow
CORNERS: With red yarn and the Log Cabin square faceup, draw up a lp in end sc (or end of sc row); ch 1.

Row 1: With RSF, sc in each sc and ch-1 sp across (or ends of sc rows). Ch 1, turn.

Row 2: With WSF, dec 1, sc across, dec 1. Ch 1, turn.

Rows 3–14: Repeat Row 2.

Row 15: With RSF, sc in first sc, ch 1, sk 1 sc, sc in last sc. Fasten off.

Work a triangle on each side of the Log Cabin square. When the last one is finished, ch 1; do not fasten off.

BORDER: Work all rounds with the Log Cabin square faceup.

Rnd 1: * Work 21 scs across side of triangle, sc in sc at corner of Log Cabin square, work 21 scs to corner. Work (sc, ch 2, sc) in corner ch-1 sp.* Repeat from * to * around. Join last sc to first. Fasten off.

With blue yarn, draw up a lp in any corner ch-2 sp; ch 1.

Rnd 2: (Sc, ch 2, sc) in ch-2 sp of corner. ** Ch 1, sk sc, sc in next sc * 11 times. Lsc around sc of Rnd 1, sc in next sc. Repeat from ** to * 11 times. (Ch 2, sc) in same corner sp. ** Repeat from ** to ** around. Join last ch to beg sc; ch 1.

Rnd 3: Sc in corner sc, (sc, ch 2, sc) in ch-2 sp, sc in next corner sc. ** Ch 1, sk ch, sc in next sc * 11 times. Ch 1, sk lsc, sc in next sc. Repeat from ** to * 11 more times. (Sc, ch 2, sc) in corner ch-2 sp, sc in next corner sc.** Repeat from ** to ** around. Join last ch to beg sc; ch 1.

Rnd 4: Sc in sc. Ch 1, sk sc, (sc, ch 2, sc) in corner ch-2 sp. Ch 1, sk sc, sc in next sc. * Ch 1, sk ch, sc in next sc 24 times. Ch 1, sk sc, (sc, ch 2, sc) in ch-2 sp of corner. Ch 1, sk sc, sc in next sc. * Repeat from * to * around. Join last ch to beg sc. Fasten off.

With red yarn, draw up a lp in any ch-1 sp on any side.

Rnd 5: (Ch 3, dc) in ch-1 sp. * (Sl st, ch 3, dc) in next ch-1 sp. * Repeat from * to * around, working (sl st, ch 3, dc) twice in each corner ch-2 sp. At end of rnd, sl st in beg ch-1 sp.

Fasten off. Weave in yarn ends on the back side, then block as needed. Finish pillow as desired.

COLOR KEY

Anchor		DMC	
002	· ·	000	white
352	⚹ ⚹	300	mahogany - vy dk
403	■ ■	310	black
147	● ●	312	navy blue - lt
399	≈ ≈	318	pearl gray - med
978	K K	322	navy blue - vy lt
059	✗ ✗	326	rose - vy dk
905	I I	645	beaver gray - dk
891	△ △	676	old gold - lt
387	∾ ∾	712	cream
326	▬ ▬	720	rust - med
323	★ ★	722	rust - lt (with 720 over it)—see instructions
323	□ □	722	rust - lt
885	+ +	739	tan - ultra vy lt
868	⊠ ⊠	758	terra cotta - lt
697	◇ ◇	762	pearl gray - vy lt
044	♥ ♥	814	garnet - dk
044	⊘ ⊘	816	garnet - med
380	⠿ ⠿	838	beige brown - vy dk
401	⋈ ⋈	844	beaver gray - vy dk
324	❖ ❖	922	copper - lt
921	⊂ ⊂	931	antique blue - med
347	J J	945	pink beige
8581	@ @	3023	brown gray - lt
903	▲ ▲	3032	mocha brown - med
914	I I	3064	pink beige - dk
379	▮ ▮	3772	rose brown - dk

Blended needle:

326	# #	720	rust - med & 002 gold KREINIK BALGER® blending filament
323	– –	722	rust - lt & 002 gold KREINIK BALGER® blending filament
891	O O	676	old gold - lt & 002 gold KREINIK BALGER® blending filament
324	H H	922	copper - lt & 002 gold KREINIK BALGER® blending filament

Backstitch:

| 403 | | 310 | everything (1 strand) |

French knot:

| 403 | ● | 310 | eyes (1 strand) |

Fabrics and finished design sizes:

11 Aida, 14-1/2"h x 9-5/8"w
14 Aida, 11-3/8"h x 7-1/2"w
18 Aida, 8-7/8"h x 5-7/8"w
22 Hardanger, 7-1/4"h x 4-7/8"w

Cross-Stitched Santa

Finished stitchery is approximately 7½x11½ inches. Stitch count is 105 wide and 159 high.

MATERIALS

18x22-inch piece of Charles Craft's 14-count Tuscan Tan Aida cloth
One skein of DMC embroidery floss in colors listed in color key, *right*
One spool of Balger gold metallic thread
Tapestry needle
Embroidery hoop

INSTRUCTIONS

Referring to the chart, *opposite,* use two strands of floss and work cross-stitches over one square of fabric.

Measure 5 inches from the top and 6½ inches from the left edge of the fabric to begin. An arrow indicates the starting point on the chart.

Work one strand of dark rust 720 over two strands of orange 722 as indicated by the keyed symbol. To stitch the ornaments, horn, and fire, blend one strand of gold metallic thread with two strands of the floss color indicated on the chart.

Work backstitches with one strand of black floss. Frame as desired.

CROSS-STITCHED SANTA

1 Square = 1 Stitch

Primitive Advent Tree

Tree is approximately 44 inches tall.

MATERIALS

One 34-inch-long, ¾-inch-diameter
   tree branch for vertical support
Assorted ½-inch-diameter branches
One 3- to 4-inch-diameter tree
   limb, cut 2 inches thick, for base
Five small twigs, each approximately 9 inches long, for the star
24 purchased twig wreaths, approximately 3 inches in diameter
Purchased ¾-inch-high wooden
   numbers 1 through 24; red paint
Assorted decorative greens, berries,
   pinecones, and dried flowers
24 small brass nails; handsaw; drill
Fine gauge wire for hanging loops
Hot-glue gun; twine

INSTRUCTIONS

Make it a family affair to count down
the days until Christmas. Starting
with No. 24 (days to go) on December 1, add a wreath to this Advent
tree every day. By Christmas Eve, it
will be completely decorated.

Making the wreaths

Paint the wooden numbers with red
paint; let dry. Glue greens and other
dried materials to the bottom of each
wreath, leaving a space for the numbers. Glue painted numbers in place.

   Twist a 2½-inch piece of wire
around twigs at the top back of each
wreath to make a hanging loop.

Making the tree

Measure 6¾ inches from the bottom
of the center branch. At this spot, saw
a notch approximately ⅝ inch wide.
Do not cut deeper than one-third the
thickness of the branch. Working up
the branch, cut six more notches
spaced about 3¼ inches apart. The
last notch will be about 3½ inches
from the top of the center branch.

   For the top crossbars, cut two
9-inch-long pieces from the ½-inch-
diameter branches. Evenly space two
wreaths on each branch to find posi-
tions for nails. Tap nails in place.

   For the remaining crossbars, place
three nails on each of two 12-inch-
long branches, four nails on each of
two 15-inch-long branches, and five
nails on one 18-inch-long branch.

   Glue crossbars into notches on the
center branch. Wrap twine around
both branches at each intersection,
tying a knot in the twine on the back
side of the tree. For added security,
add glue to knot.

   For the top wreath, drive a nail
halfway into the center branch, placing it a scant ½ inch from the top.

   Drill a hole in the center of the
base large enough to accept the vertical branch of the tree. Insert branch;
add glue to secure it.

   Arrange five twigs in a star shape;
glue and tie intersections together.
Glue star to top of tree.

Festive Treats
FROM THE KITCHEN

During this cozy season, warm the hearts of others by sharing with them a holiday treat from your kitchen. Take a tasty cheeseball, cover it with a festive wrap, and tie on a pretty cheese spreader. Or, pack a jar of homemade spaghetti sauce in a basket with all the makings for a great dinner.

Look for these and other food gift ideas within this section. Use the photos as a guide and adapt the ideas to your liking. The recipe directions are easy to follow and make-ahead storage tips let you plan ahead to avoid the holiday hassles.

Raspberry Vinegar

1½ **cups fresh red raspberries** *or*
½ **of a 12-ounce package**
frozen lightly sweetened
red raspberries (1½ cups)
2 **cups white vinegar**
1 **cup dry white wine**
Fresh raspberries (optional)

🎁 If using *fresh* raspberries, thoroughly rinse the raspberries with cold water. Drain well. In a stainless steel or enamel saucepan bring the 1½ cups fresh or frozen raspberries, the vinegar, and white wine to boiling. Boil gently, uncovered, for 3 minutes. Remove from heat and cool slightly.

🎁 Pour the hot raspberry mixture into a hot, clean 1-quart jar. Cover *loosely* with a glass, plastic, or cork lid (the vinegar will corrode metal lids). Let the jar stand till the mixture cools completely. Then, cover the jar *tightly* with the non-metal lid. Let vinegar stand in a cool, dark place for 1 week.

🎁 After 1 week, line a colander with fine-woven cloth, 100 percent cotton cheesecloth, or a cup-shaped coffee filter. Pour the raspberry mixture through the colander and let it drain into a bowl. Transfer the strained vinegar to a clean 1½-pint bottle or jar. If desired, add a few fresh raspberries to the bottle or jar for easier identification. Cover the bottle or jar tightly with a glass, plastic, or cork lid. Makes about 3 cups.

*T*o store: Prepare Raspberry Vinegar as directed above. Label and refrigerate for up to 6 months.

Herb Vinegar

2 **cups tightly packed fresh**
herb leaves *or* **sprigs**
(tarragon, thyme, dill,
basil, *or* **mint)**
2 **cups white vinegar**
Fresh herb sprig (optional)

🎁 Pack 2 cups herbs into a hot, clean 1-quart jar. In a stainless steel or enamel saucepan heat vinegar till hot, *but not boiling*.

🎁 Pour hot vinegar over herbs in jar. Cover *loosely* with a glass, plastic, or cork lid (the vinegar will corrode metal lids). Let jar stand till the mixture cools completely. Then, cover the jar *tightly* with the non-metal lid. Let vinegar stand in a cool, dark place for 1 week.

🎁 After 1 week, remove herbs from jar. Transfer vinegar to a clean 1½-pint bottle or jar. If desired, add a sprig of fresh herb to the bottle or jar for easier identification. Cover tightly with a glass, plastic, or cork lid. Makes 2 cups.

*T*o store: Prepare Herb Vinegar as directed above. Label and place in a cool, dark place for up to 6 months.

Marinated Cheese

- 2 8-ounce blocks mozzarella, Monterey Jack, *or* cheddar cheese
- 3 small red, green, *and/or* yellow sweet peppers, seeded
- 1 2¼-ounce can sliced pitted ripe olives, drained (optional)
- 1 8-ounce bottle (1 cup) clear Italian salad dressing

🎁 Cut the cheese into ½-inch-thick slices. Using 1-inch cutters, cut the cheese into moon and star shapes. Using a 1-inch cutter, cut the peppers into star shapes. (*Or,* using a knife, cut the peppers into ¾- to 1-inch squares or triangles, or 1-inch-long strips.)

🎁 Place cheese; red, green, and/or yellow peppers; and, if desired, olives in a 1- to 1½-quart clear jar or container with a tight-fitting lid. Pour salad dressing over mixture in the jar or container. Cover and gently turn jar or container to coat cheese mixture with dressing. Marinate cheese mixture in the refrigerator for 1 week before using, gently turning jar or container occasionally.

🎁 To serve, let the cheese mixture stand at room temperature for 30 minutes. Using a slotted spoon, transfer the cheese and peppers to a bowl. Serve as an appetizer with decorative picks. Makes 3½ cups.

To store: Prepare the Marinated Cheese as directed above. Label and marinate the cheese mixture in the refrigerator for up to 1 month, gently turning container occasionally.

Fruit Juice Jelly

If you make the orange juice jelly, allow 2 weeks for the jelly to set.

4 **cups unsweetened orange, grape,** *or* **apple juice,** *or* **cranberry juice cocktail (not low-calorie)**

¼ **cup lemon juice**

1 **1¾-ounce package powdered fruit pectin**

4½ **cups sugar**

🎁 In an 8- or 10-quart Dutch oven stir together the fruit juice and lemon juice. Sprinkle with pectin. Let the pectin stand for 1 to 2 minutes. Then, stir the pectin into the juice mixture to dissolve it.

🎁 Bring the juice mixture to a full rolling boil over medium-high heat, stirring frequently. Stir in the sugar. Return to a full rolling boil, stirring frequently. Then, boil hard for 1 minute, stirring constantly. Remove the Dutch oven from the heat. *Immediately* skim the foam off the juice mixture using a metal spoon.

🎁 Ladle the juice mixture into hot, *sterilized* half-pint jars, leaving a ¼-inch headspace. Adjust lids. Process in a boiling-water canner for 5 minutes. Makes 6 half-pints.

***T*o store:** Prepare Fruit Juice Jelly as directed above. Label and store sealed jars at room temperature for up to 1 year.

Cornmeal Biscuit Mix

- 1½ cups all-purpose flour
- ½ cup yellow cornmeal
- 2 teaspoons baking powder
- ⅛ to ¼ teaspoon ground red pepper (optional)
- ½ cup margarine *or* butter
- ½ cup shredded cheddar cheese (2 ounces)

In a medium mixing bowl stir together the flour, cornmeal, baking powder, and, if desired, red pepper. Using a pastry blender, cut in the margarine or butter till mixture resembles coarse crumbs. Stir in the cheese. Use mix to prepare Cornmeal Biscuits. Makes 1 recipe (3 cups) mix.

Cornmeal Biscuits: Place 1 recipe *Cornmeal Biscuit Mix* in a medium mixing bowl. Make a well in the center of the dry mixture. Add ⅔ cup *milk* all at once to the dry mixture. Using a fork, stir *just till moistened.* Turn the dough out onto a lightly floured surface. Quickly knead the dough by gently folding and pressing it for 10 to 12 strokes or till dough is *nearly* smooth. Pat or lightly roll dough to ½-inch thickness. Cut the dough with a floured 2½-inch biscuit cutter, dipping the cutter into flour between cuts. Place biscuits on an ungreased baking sheet. Bake in a 450° oven for 12 to 15 minutes or till golden. Remove biscuits from baking sheet and serve hot. Makes 10 to 12 biscuits.

To store: Prepare Cornmeal Biscuit Mix as directed above. Transfer biscuit mix to a plastic bag or container. Seal, label, and refrigerate for up to 2 weeks.

Choose-a-Bean Soup Mix

- 3 tablespoons dried minced onion
- 2 tablespoons wheat berries
- 2 tablespoons pearl barley
- 2 tablespoons celery flakes
- 1 tablespoon instant beef bouillon granules
- ½ teaspoon dried basil, crushed
- ¼ cup dry garbanzo beans
- ¼ cup dry red kidney beans *or* pinto beans
- ¼ cup dry navy beans *or* lima beans
- ¼ cup dry split *or* whole green peas
- 1 bay leaf

For seasoning mixture, in a custard cup stir together dried onion, wheat berries, pearl barley, celery flakes, bouillon granules, and basil.

To assemble, transfer seasoning mixture to a 1-pint jar, or small cellophane or plastic bag. Layer the garbanzo beans; red kidney or pinto beans; navy or lima beans; and peas on top the seasoning. Place bay leaf on top. Cover jar or seal bag tightly. Use mix to prepare Meaty Vegetable Soup. Makes 1 recipe (2 cups) mix.

Meaty Vegetable Soup: In a 4-quart Dutch oven combine 1 recipe *Choose-a-Bean Soup Mix* and 6 cups *water.* Bring to boiling; reduce heat. Cover and simmer for 2 minutes. Remove from heat and let stand, covered, for 1 hour. (*Or,* in a covered Dutch oven soak soup mix in the 6 cups water overnight. *Do not drain.*)

Add 1 pound smoked *pork hocks* or *beef shank crosscuts* to the beans. Bring to boiling, then reduce heat. Cover and simmer for 1½ hours.

Remove pork hocks or beef shank crosscuts from Dutch oven. When meat is cool enough to handle, remove the meat from bones and coarsely chop it. Discard the bones. Remove and discard bay leaf from soup.

Return the chopped meat to the Dutch oven. Add one 16-ounce can *undrained tomatoes;* 1 medium *carrot,* cut up; and ⅛ teaspoon *garlic powder.* Cover and simmer soup for 30 minutes. If desired, season to taste with salt. Ladle the soup into soup bowls. Makes 6 main-dish servings.

To store: Assemble the Choose-a-Bean Soup Mix package as directed above. Label and place soup mix in a cool, dry place for up to 9 months.

Pop-the-Cork Pasta Crunch

1 **7-ounce package corkscrew macaroni (2¾ cups)**
⅓ **cup grated Parmesan cheese**
½ **teaspoon Italian seasoning, crushed**
¼ **teaspoon garlic salt**
   Cooking oil for deep-fat frying

❧ Cook the macaroni according to package directions. Drain in a colander. Rinse pasta with cold water, then drain well. Using paper towels, pat excess moisture from cooked pasta. Let pasta dry in a single layer about 3 hours or till pasta feels dry when touched.

❧ In a small bowl stir together the Parmesan cheese, Italian seasoning, and garlic salt. Set the cheese mixture aside.

❧ In a deep-fat fryer heat 1½ inches of cooking oil to 365°. Carefully fry pasta, *about 12 at a time*, in the hot oil about 1 minute or till lightly brown, stirring to separate after 30 seconds of cooking. Using a slotted spoon, remove pasta from oil. Drain pasta on paper towels.

❧ While the pasta is still warm, sprinkle with the cheese mixture. Gently toss till coated. Cool. Makes 10 (½-cup) servings.

*T*o store: Prepare Pop-the-Cork Pasta Crunch as directed above. Transfer to a freezer bag or container. Seal, label, and freeze for up to 6 months or place in a cool, dry place for up to 1 week. If frozen, thaw the fried pasta at room temperature about 10 minutes before packaging.

Crunchy Caramel Snack Mix

Load a dozen little bags with this crunchy mix or with Gingered Nuts. Pack the bags in a hatbox to give to a friend who then can enjoy a bag of goodies on each of the 12 days of Christmas.

3 cups chocolate-flavored puffed corn cereal
3 cups bite-size rice square cereal
2 cups small twisted pretzels
1 cup peanuts
1 cup packed brown sugar
½ cup margarine *or* butter
¼ cup light corn syrup
¼ teaspoon baking soda
¼ teaspoon cream of tartar
½ teaspoon vanilla

❖ In a 13x9x2-inch baking pan combine the chocolate-flavored corn cereal, rice cereal, pretzels, and peanuts. Set aside.

❖ For syrup, in a medium saucepan combine the brown sugar, margarine or butter, and corn syrup. Cook and stir over medium heat till margarine melts and mixture begins to boil. Then, over medium heat, cook without stirring for 4 minutes.

❖ Remove saucepan from heat and stir in baking soda and cream of tartar. Then, stir in vanilla. Pour syrup over cereal mixture, stirring till cereal is coated with syrup.

❖ Bake mixture in a 300° oven 30 minutes, stirring after 15 minutes. Transfer to a larger shallow baking pan; cool. Makes about 10 cups.

To store: Prepare Crunchy Caramel Snack Mix as directed above. Transfer the cooled mix to a container. Seal, label, and place in a cool, dry place for up to 3 days.

Ginger Nuts

1 egg white
1 teaspoon *cold* water
1 pound lightly salted mixed nuts
½ cup sugar
1 teaspoon grated lemon peel
1 teaspoon grated gingerroot

❖ In a medium mixing bowl beat the egg white with the cold water till frothy. Add the mixed nuts and stir till well combined.

❖ In a small mixing bowl stir together the sugar, lemon peel, and gingerroot. Pour the sugar mixture over the nut mixture. Toss till the nuts are evenly coated. Spread the nuts in a single layer in a greased 15x10x1-inch baking pan.

❖ Bake nuts in a 300° oven for 20 minutes, stirring after 10 minutes. Stir again when you remove them from the oven. Cool nuts in pan, stirring once. Makes 3 cups.

To store: Prepare Ginger Nuts as directed above. Transfer nuts to a plastic bag or container. Seal, label, and place in a cool, dry place for up to 2 weeks.

Chutney Cheese Ball

2 cups shredded sharp cheddar cheese (8 ounces)
1 8-ounce package cream cheese
2 tablespoons margarine *or* butter
⅓ cup finely snipped chutney
1 teaspoon Worcestershire sauce
   Dash bottled hot pepper sauce
½ cup finely chopped toasted pecans *or* peanuts

🎁 Bring the cheddar cheese, cream cheese, and margarine or butter to room temperature.

🎁 In a medium mixing bowl beat the cheddar cheese and margarine or butter with an electric mixer till combined. Add cream cheese, chutney, Worcestershire sauce, and hot pepper sauce. Beat till thoroughly combined. Cover and refrigerate for 3 to 24 hours.

🎁 Shape the chilled cheese mixture into 1 large ball or 2 small balls. Then roll the cheese ball(s) in pecans or peanuts. Serve with crackers. Makes 1 large or 2 small cheese balls.

To store: Mix and shape Chutney Cheese Ball(s) as directed above. *Do not roll ball(s) in nuts.* Tightly wrap the cheese ball in plastic wrap. Label and refrigerate cheese ball for up to 5 days *or* freeze for up to 1 month. If frozen, thaw the wrapped cheese ball(s) in the refrigerator for 10 to 12 hours. Roll the cheese ball(s) in nuts before packaging.

Blaze-of-Glory Salsa

1 **28-ounce can tomatoes, drained, seeded, and finely chopped**
3 **tablespoons finely chopped onion**
3 **tablespoons finely chopped green sweet pepper**
3 **tablespoons finely chopped jalapeño pepper***
1 **tablespoon snipped fresh cilantro *or* 1 teaspoon dried cilantro, crushed**
1 **tablespoon red wine vinegar**
2 **cloves garlic, minced**
¼ **teaspoon salt**
   Several dashes bottled hot pepper sauce
   Wonton Stars

Combine the tomatoes, onion, green pepper, jalapeño pepper, cilantro, vinegar, garlic, salt, hot pepper sauce, and dash *pepper*.

Transfer salsa to a container. Seal and refrigerate for 3 to 8 hours, stirring occasionally. Serve with Wonton Stars. Makes about 1½ cups sauce.

* Because chili peppers contain volatile oils that can burn your skin and eyes, avoid direct contact with the jalapeño pepper as much as possible. Wear plastic or rubber gloves or work under cold running water. If your bare hands touch the peppers, wash your hands and nails well with soap and water.

Wonton Stars: Stir together ¼ cup melted *margarine* or *butter*, ¾ teaspoon *dry mustard*, ¾ teaspoon *onion powder*, ¾ teaspoon *garlic salt*, and ⅛ teaspoon ground *red pepper*.
Separate one 16-ounce package *wonton skins*. Place wonton skins in a single layer on baking sheets sprayed with *nonstick spray coating*. To shape the skins into stars, cut

1-inch slits from each corner to the center of *each* square. Fold every other point to the center to form a star. Moisten center with water and press points in place. *Or*, using a cookie cutter cut wonton skins into star shapes. Brush with margarine mixture. Sprinkle with *paprika* or grated *Parmesan cheese*.
Bake in a 350° oven for 8 to 10 minutes or till crisp and golden brown. Remove stars and cool on a wire rack. Makes about 48 stars.

To store: Prepare Blaze-of-Glory Salsa and Wonton Stars as directed above. Label and refrigerate salsa for up to 2 weeks. Transfer cooled chips to a container. Seal, label, and freeze for up to 6 months or place in a cool, dry place for up to 1 week. Thaw frozen chips at room temperature about 10 minutes before packaging.

Hazelnut Muffins

1¾ cups all-purpose flour
⅔ cup chopped hazelnuts (filberts) *or* pecans, toasted
¼ cup sugar
2 teaspoons baking powder
½ teaspoon salt
1 beaten egg
¾ cup milk
⅓ cup cooking oil
⅓ cup chopped hazelnuts (filberts) *or* pecans
 Chocolate Butter *or* soft-style cream cheese

Grease five 3½-inch muffin cups (or twelve 2½-inch muffin cups) or line them with paper bake cups. Set muffin cups aside.

In a large mixing bowl stir together the flour, the ⅔ cup toasted nuts, sugar, baking powder, and salt. Make a well in the center of the dry mixture.

In a medium mixing bowl combine the egg, milk, and cooking oil. Add the egg mixture all at once to the dry mixture. Stir *just till moistened* (batter should be lumpy).

Spoon the batter into the prepared muffin cups, filling each full. Sprinkle muffins with the ⅓ cup nuts. Bake the 3½-inch muffins in a 350° oven for 25 to 27 minutes (or the 2½-inch muffins in a 400° oven for 18 to 20 minutes) or till golden. Remove the muffins from the muffin cups and cool on wire racks. Serve with Chocolate Butter or cream cheese. Makes 5 (3½-inch) or 12 (2½-inch) muffins.

Chocolate Butter: In a heavy small saucepan or skillet melt ¼ cup *semisweet chocolate pieces* and 1 tablespoon *butter* or *margarine* over low heat, stirring occasionally. Remove from the heat and cool about 5 minutes.

In a small mixing bowl stir together ½ cup softened *butter* or *margarine*, ½ teaspoon *vanilla*, and the melted chocolate mixture. If desired, spoon the butter mixture into a decorating bag fitted with a medium star tip. Pipe the butter into small candy cups. Makes ¾ cup.

*T*o store: Prepare and bake Hazelnut Muffins as directed above. Cool completely. Wrap muffins tightly in *heavy* foil or place them in freezer bags. Seal, label, and freeze for up to 3 months. Thaw wrapped muffins at room temperature about 1 hour for 3½-inch muffins (or about 30 minutes for 2½-inch muffins) before packaging.

Prepare Chocolate Butter as directed above. Transfer to a freezer container. Seal, label, and freeze for up to 2 months or refrigerate for up to 2 weeks. Let butter stand at room temperature about 1 hour before packaging.

Bready Bears

1 28-ounce package frozen
  sweet bread dough
  (2 loaves)
1 beaten egg white
  Powdered Sugar Glaze
  Candied *or* dried fruit, cut
  up, *or* chopped nuts

Thaw dough. According to the package directions, let the dough rise in a warm place till it is double in size. Punch down loaves. Cover and let rest 10 minutes.

On a lightly floured surface, roll *1 loaf* to ¼-inch thickness. Use round cutters to cut *five* 2½-inch circles; *five* 2-inch circles; and *twenty-five* 1-inch circles. (For easier rolling, let dough rest about 10 minutes before rerolling.) Combine egg white and 1 tablespoon *water*.

To assemble *each* bear, place *one* 2½-inch circle (for the body) on a greased baking sheet. For the head, brush the side of *one* 2-inch circle with egg white mixture; join to body. For arms and legs, brush the sides of *four* 1-inch circles with egg white mixture; join to body. For ears, cut *one* 1-inch circle in half. Brush egg white on the flat side of each half; join to head. Repeat, making bears with remaining loaf.

Cover the bears and let them rise in a warm place about 20 minutes or till *nearly* double in size. Uncover and bake in a 375° oven 10 to 12 minutes or till lightly brown. Cool slightly on a wire rack. Brush the bears with Powdered Sugar Glaze and decorate with fruit or nuts. Makes 10.

Powdered Sugar Glaze: In a small mixing bowl stir together 2 cups sifted *powdered sugar*, ¼ cup *hot water*, and 1 teaspoon *margarine or butter*. Makes 1 cup.

Candy Name Tags

12 ounces chocolate- *or* vanilla-
  flavored *or* colored candy
  coating, melted
  Several drops oil of
  peppermint *or* cinnamon
  (*not extract*) (optional)
4 ounces vanilla- *or* chocolate-
  flavored *or* colored candy
  coating, melted
  Assorted ribbon

Line a baking sheet with waxed paper; set aside. If desired, stir enough oil of peppermint into the 12 ounces of melted coating to suit taste. Pour the mixture onto the prepared baking sheet, spreading to ⅛- to ¼-inch thickness. Refrigerate about 5 minutes or till *nearly* set, checking *every minute* so coating does not become too firm to cut.

Using 2-inch cutters, cut the partially set candy coating into desired shapes. Using a plastic straw, cut a hole in the top of each cutout. Chill till firm. Spoon a contrasting color of melted candy coating into a decorating bag fitted with a small round tip. If necessary, cool slightly. Pipe a name and, if desired, a decorative border or design on each cutout. Chill till firm. Remove cutouts from baking sheet and string a small piece of ribbon through each hole. Tie candy tag onto a package. Makes 9.

*T*o store: Assemble and bake Bready Bears as directed. *Do not glaze or decorate with fruit.* Cool completely; wrap tightly in *heavy* foil or place in a freezer bag or container. Seal, label, and freeze for up to 3 months. Thaw wrapped bears at room temperature about 1 hour. Brush with glaze and decorate before packaging.

Prepare Candy Name Tags as directed above. Place in a container. Seal, label, and place in a cool, dry place for up to 1 month.

Christmas Tree Bread

1 **14-ounce loaf frozen sweet bread dough** *or* **one 16-ounce loaf frozen white** *or* **whole wheat bread dough**
Powdered Sugar Icing
Small gumdrops, sliced

🎁 Thaw dough according to package directions. *Do not let dough rise.* Divide dough into *17* pieces. Shape *15* of the pieces into 1½-inch balls, pulling dough under to make smooth tops. (Set remaining 2 pieces aside.)

🎁 To assemble the tree, on a greased baking sheet place shaped balls in a tree shape, starting with a row of 5 balls, followed by rows of 4, 3, 2, and 1 balls. Combine the remaining 2 pieces into 1 larger ball. Slightly flatten the larger ball and place it at the base of the tree.

🎁 Cover dough and let it rise in a warm place about 20 minutes or till dough is *nearly* double in size. Uncover and bake in a 375° oven about 20 minutes or till lightly brown, covering with foil during the last 5 minutes of baking to prevent overbrowning. Carefully remove the bread from the baking sheet and cool on a wire rack.

🎁 To decorate, drizzle bread tree with Powdered Sugar Icing and garnish with gumdrops. Makes 1 tree-shaped loaf.

Powdered Sugar Icing: In a small mixing bowl stir together 1 cup sifted *powdered sugar,* ¼ teaspoon *vanilla,* and enough *milk* or *orange juice* to make icing of drizzling consistency. Makes ½ cup.

*T*o store: Assemble and bake the Christmas Tree Bread as directed above. *Do not frost or decorate with gumdrops.* Cool completely. Wrap the bread tightly in *heavy* foil or place it in a freezer bag or container. Seal, label, and freeze for up to 3 months. Thaw the wrapped bread at room temperature about 1 hour. Drizzle with icing and decorate with gumdrops before packaging.

Sugar Cookie Cutout Cards

⅓ cup shortening
⅓ cup margarine *or* butter
2 cups all-purpose flour
¾ cup sugar
1 egg
1 tablespoon milk
1 teaspoon baking powder
1 teaspoon vanilla
 Finely crushed clear hard candy

❚❚ In a large mixing bowl beat the shortening and margarine or butter with an electric mixer on medium to high speed about 30 seconds or till softened.
❚❚ Add about *half* the flour, the sugar, egg, milk, baking powder, vanilla, and dash *salt* to the shortening. Beat till thoroughly combined, scraping the sides of the bowl occasionally. Beat or stir in remaining flour. Divide dough in half. Cover and chill about 3 hours or till easy to handle.
❚❚ On a large cookie sheet lined with foil, roll *each* portion of dough to ⅛-inch thickness. Measure the inside of a shallow vase or flat gift

box. Cut the dough to the size of the inside of vase or box, leaving 1 inch between cookies. Remove dough scraps. Using ¾- to 1-inch alphabet or other desired cutters, cut out a message and/or design in the dough. Remove dough scraps. Fill each hole with candy.
❚❚ Bake cookies in a 375° oven for 7 to 8 minutes or till edges are firm and bottoms are light brown. Transfer cookies on foil to a wire rack to cool. After cookies cool, carefully remove foil. Makes 4 (7½-inch-square) cookies.

*T*o store: Prepare Sugar Cookie Cutout Cards as directed above. Transfer the cookies to individual freezer bags or containers. Seal, label, and freeze for up to 6 months. Open bags or containers and thaw at room temperature about 15 minutes before packaging.

Gingerbread Spritz

    1   11-ounce package piecrust
          mix (for a 2-crust pie)
    ½   cup sugar
    1   teaspoon ground cinnamon
    ½   teaspoon ground ginger
    ½   teaspoon ground nutmeg
    ½   teaspoon grated orange peel
    ¼   cup water
    2   tablespoons molasses
        Small multicolored
          decorative candies *and/or*
          colored sugars (optional)

🎁 In a large mixing bowl stir together piecrust mix, sugar, cinnamon, ginger, nutmeg, and orange peel till well combined.

🎁 Stir together the water and molasses. Add molasses mixture to the dry ingredients. Stir till moistened and thoroughly combined. *Do not chill dough.*

🎁 Pack dough into a cookie press. Force dough through the press onto an ungreased cookie sheet. Decorate cookies with candies and/or colored sugars. Bake in a 375° oven 8 to 10 minutes or till edges are firm. Remove from cookie sheet and cool on a wire rack. Makes about 50 cookies.

To store: Prepare Gingerbread Spritz and Gift-Giving Cookie Bowl, *except* do not decorate bowl. Transfer cookies and bowl to separate freezer bags or containers. Seal, label, and freeze for up to 6 months. Open bags; thaw at room temperature 15 minutes. Decorate bowl and fill with cookies.

Gift-Giving Cookie Bowl

        Dough for Sugar Cookie
          Cutout Cards *(see recipe,
          page 93)*
    ¼   cup all-purpose flour
        Frosting (optional)
        Cookies

🎁 Prepare cookie dough for Sugar-Cookie Cutout Cards as directed. Divide the dough in half. Cover and chill dough about 3 hours or till easy to handle.

🎁 Meanwhile, invert a 1- or 1½-quart ovenproof bowl or round casserole in a shallow baking pan. Cover the ovenproof bowl or casserole with foil. Grease the foil. Set aside. For a pattern, cut out a 9-inch circle from paper. Set aside.

🎁 For *one* Gift-Giving Cookie Bowl, use *one portion* of dough (use the remaining dough for Sugar Cookie Cutout Cards or another cookie bowl). Knead flour into the dough being used for the bowl.

🎁 Between 2 sheets of waxed paper, roll the cookie dough into an 11-inch circle. Remove the top sheet of waxed paper. Place the 9-inch circle paper pattern on top of the dough. Using a fluted or plain pastry cutter, cut around the pattern. Remove the paper pattern from the dough. If desired, use ¾-inch or 1-inch cutters to cut out decorative shapes from the scraps of dough. Transfer the decorative shapes to another cookie sheet and set aside.

🎁 Invert the dough circle with the waxed paper and place it on the inverted ovenproof bowl or casserole. Remove the waxed paper and form dough over the bowl.

🎁 Bake the cookie bowl in a 350° oven about 15 minutes or till edge is very light brown. Transfer cookie bowl on the inverted ovenproof bowl or casserole to a wire rack to cool. Then, carefully remove the cookie bowl from the ovenproof bowl or casserole.

🎁 Bake the decorative shapes in the 350° oven about 6 minutes or till edges are light brown. Remove the shapes from the cookie sheet and cool on a wire rack. Attach the shapes to the cookie bowl with desired frosting. Decorate bowl as desired. Fill cookie bowl with cookies. Makes 1 bowl plus additional cookies or another bowl.

Gift-Giving Cookie Pops

1 cup margarine *or* butter
1 8-ounce package cream cheese, softened
3½ cups all-purpose flour
2 cups sugar
1 egg
1 teaspoon baking powder
1 teaspoon vanilla
⅓ cup small multicolored decorative candies *or* multicolored crystal sugar
Wooden sticks *or* lollipop sticks
¼ cup margarine *or* butter, softened
¼ cup all-purpose flour
1 tablespoon strawberry-flavored syrup, crème-de-menthe-flavored syrup, *or* grenadine
Red *or* green food coloring (optional)

🎁 In a mixing bowl beat 1 cup margarine or butter and cream cheese with an electric mixer on medium to high speed about 30 seconds or till softened.

🎁 Add about *half* of the 3½ cups flour, the 2 cups sugar, egg, baking powder, and vanilla to the margarine mixture. Beat till thoroughly combined, scraping sides of bowl occasionally. Then beat or stir in the remaining flour and the decorative candies or multicolored crystal sugar. Divide dough in half. Cover and chill for 3 to 24 hours or till easy to handle.

🎁 On a lightly floured surface, roll *each* portion of dough to ⅜-inch thickness. Cut into 2½- to 3½-inch shapes (such as hearts, flowers, or shamrocks). Place cookie shapes 1 inch apart on a cookie sheet. Push a stick into one side near the center of *each* cookie (the dough should cover the stick). If necessary, press dough down slightly so that the cookie bakes around the stick.

🎁 In a small mixing bowl stir together the ¼ cup softened margarine or butter; the ¼ cup all-purpose flour; strawberry-flavored syrup, crème-de-menthe-flavored syrup or grenadine; and, if desired, a few drops of food coloring. Stir till smooth. Spoon the mixture into a small, heavy plastic bag. Snip off one corner of the bag. (Or, use a decorating bag fitted with a small round tip.) Pipe mixture onto cutout dough in desired designs.

🎁 Bake cookies in a 350° oven for 12 to 15 minutes or till edges are firm and bottoms are very lightly browned. Carefully, remove cookies from cookie sheet and cool on a wire rack. Makes about 36 (3½-inch) cookies or 48 (2½-inch) cookies.

*T*o store: Prepare Gift-Giving Cookie Pops. Transfer cookies to a freezer bag or container. Seal, label, and freeze for up to 6 months. Open bag or container and thaw at room temperature about 15 minutes before packaging.

Caramel-and-Chocolate-Dipped Apples

Dash down to the candy store to find top quality, great-tasting candy coating for dipping these yummy apples.

6 **extra-large apples (4 pounds)**
6 **wooden sticks**
21 **ounces (about 75) vanilla caramels** *or* **chocolate caramels**
3 **tablespoons water**
3 **cups coarsely chopped pecans, cashews, macadamia nuts,** *or* **almonds**
18 **ounces milk chocolate** *or* **semisweet chocolate bar, white baking bar with cocoa butter,** *or* **chocolate- or vanilla-flavored candy coating, chopped**
3 **tablespoons shortening**
Small multicolored decorative candies *or* **colored sugar (optional)**
6 **ounces milk chocolate** *or* **semisweet chocolate bars, white baking bars with cocoa butter,** *or* **colored candy coating, chopped (optional)**
1 **tablespoon shortening (optional)**
6 **5- to 6-inch-long candy canes (optional)**

Wash and dry apples. Remove stems. Insert *one* wooden stick into the stem end of *each* apple. Set the apples aside.

In a heavy medium saucepan heat and stir the *unwrapped* caramels and water over medium-low heat just till caramels are melted. Dip each apple into the hot caramel mixture, spooning caramel evenly over apple. Allow excess caramel to drip off. Immediately roll apples in nuts. Place apples, bottom sides down, on waxed paper and let them stand 25 minutes or till firm.

In another heavy medium saucepan heat and stir the 18 ounces chocolate, white baking bar, or chocolate- or vanilla-flavored candy coating and the 3 tablespoons shortening over low heat just till mixture is melted. Holding apples over the saucepan, spoon the melted chocolate evenly

over the caramel-and-nut-coated apples. Allow excess chocolate to drip off. Place apples, bottom sides down, on waxed paper.

If desired, immediately sprinkle apples with decorative candies or colored sugar. *Or,* let apples stand about 1 hour till chocolate is firm. If desired, in a small saucepan heat the 6 ounces chocolate, white baking bar, or candy coating and the 1 tablespoon shortening. Then, drizzle apples with melted chocolate or colored candy coating and let stand till firm. If desired, remove wooden sticks and carefully insert candy canes into apples. Makes 6 dipped apples.

Peanutty Caramel-and-Chocolate-Dipped Apples: Prepare Caramel-and-Chocolate-Dipped Apples as directed above, *except* stir ¼ cup *peanut butter* into the melted vanilla or chocolate caramels (if mixture is too thick, stir in an additional 2 to 3 teaspoons *water*). Use 3 cups coarsely chopped cocktail *peanuts* for the chopped nuts.

*T*o store: Prepare Caramel-and-Chocolate-Dipped Apples or Peanutty Caramel-and-Chocolate-Dipped Apples as directed above. When chocolate or colored candy coating is firm, wrap the apples in plastic or place them in a container. Seal, label, and refrigerate for up to 2 weeks.

Before packaging, remove plastic wrap, if it was used. If desired, remove wooden sticks and insert candy canes before packaging.

Shortcut Cappuccino Caramels

1 cup margarine *or* butter
1 16-ounce package (2¼ cups packed) brown sugar
1 14-ounce can (1¼ cups) *sweetened condensed* milk
1 cup light corn syrup
3 tablespoons instant coffee crystals
1 cup chopped walnuts
1 teaspoon vanilla
½ to 1 teaspoon finely shredded orange peel
64 *or* 81 small walnut halves *or* chocolate-covered coffee bean candies (optional)

▮▮ Line an 8x8x2-inch or a 9x9x2-inch baking pan with foil, extending foil over edges of pan. Butter the foil; set pan aside.

▮▮ In a heavy 3-quart saucepan melt the margarine or butter over low heat. Stir in the brown sugar, sweetened condensed milk, corn syrup, and coffee crystals. Carefully clip a candy thermometer to the side of the saucepan.

▮▮ Cook over medium heat, stirring frequently, till the thermometer registers 248° or candy reaches firm-ball stage*. Mixture should boil at a moderate, steady rate over the entire surface. Reaching firm-ball stage should take 15 to 20 minutes.

▮▮ Remove the saucepan from the heat. Remove the candy thermometer from the saucepan. Immediately stir in the 1 cup chopped walnuts, vanilla, and orange peel. Quickly pour the caramel mixture into the prepared baking pan. If desired, place walnut halves or chocolate coffee beans 1 inch apart on top of caramel. Press the walnut halves or chocolate coffee beans slightly into the caramel.

▮▮ When caramel is firm, use foil to lift it out of the pan. Use a buttered knife to cut the caramel into squares, cutting between the walnut halves or chocolate coffee beans.

Wrap each caramel piece in confectioners' foil or in clear plastic wrap. Makes 64 or 81 pieces or about 3 pounds.

* To test the candy for firm-ball stage, drop a few drops of the caramel mixture into a custard cup of *very cold water*. Shape the drops of the caramel mixture into a ball. When the caramel ball is removed from the water, it will be firm enough to hold its shape, but should quickly flatten at room temperature.

*T*o store: Prepare and wrap Shortcut Cappuccino Caramels as directed above. Place caramels in a freezer container. Seal, label, and freeze for up to 9 months. Thaw, covered, at room temperature about 1 hour before packaging.

Freezer Tomato Sauce

6 pounds plum tomatoes *or* **regular tomatoes**
1½ cups chopped onion
½ cup chopped celery
3 large cloves garlic, minced
2 tablespoons olive oil *or* **cooking oil**
2 teaspoons sugar
1 to 2 teaspoons salt
½ teaspoon pepper
1 cayenne chili pepper*, seeded and finely chopped (½ teaspoon) *or* **⅛ teaspoon ground red pepper**
2 tablespoons snipped fresh oregano *or* **2 teaspoons dried oregano, crushed**
1 to 2 tablespoons snipped fresh thyme *or* **1 to 2 teaspoons dried thyme, crushed**

In a Dutch oven bring 4 inches of *water* to boiling. Immerse tomatoes in boiling water for 1 minute. Transfer to cold water. Peel, seed, and chop tomatoes. (You should have about 10 cups.)

In the Dutch oven cook onion, celery, and garlic in hot oil about 5 minutes or till tender. Add the tomatoes, sugar, salt, pepper, and, cayenne pepper or ground red pepper. Bring to boiling, then reduce heat. Simmer, uncovered, for 45 minutes, stirring occasionally. Stir in the oregano and thyme. Simmer, uncovered, for 15 minutes more. Cool slightly.

Place *one-fourth* of the mixture in a food processor bowl. Cover and process sauce to desired texture. (Or, put mixture through a food mill.) Transfer the pureed mixture to a large bowl set in *ice water* to cool mixture quickly. Process and chill remaining mixture, one-fourth at a time.

Transfer sauce to 1-pint or 1-quart freezer containers or straight-sided canning jars. Seal, label, and freeze for up to 6 months.

To serve, transfer sauce to a saucepan and heat over medium heat till hot, stirring occasionally. Serve sauce over cooked pasta. Makes 3 to 4 pints sauce.

* Because chili peppers contain volatile oils that can burn your skin and eyes, avoid direct contact with the cayenne pepper as much as possible. Wear plastic or rubber gloves. If your bare hands do touch the peppers, wash your hands and nails well with soap and water.

Homemade Dog Biscuits

    1 **package active dry yeast**
    ¼ **cup** *warm* **water (110° to
       115°)**
    1 **cup** *warm* **chicken broth
       (110° to 115°)**
    2 **tablespoons molasses**
  1¾ **to 2 cups all-purpose flour**
  1½ **cups whole wheat flour**
    1 **cup cracked wheat**
    ½ **cup cornmeal**
    ½ **cup nonfat dry milk powder**
    2 **teaspoons salt**
    2 **teaspoons garlic powder**
    1 **beaten egg**
    1 **tablespoon milk**

▌▌ In a large bowl dissolve yeast in
the warm water. Stir in the warm
chicken broth and molasses. Then
stir in *1 cup* of the all-purpose flour,
the whole wheat flour, cracked
wheat, cornmeal, dry milk, salt, and
garlic powder. Mix well.

▌▌ Turn the dough out onto a
floured surface. Knead in enough
of the remaining flour to make a
very stiff dough (10 to 12 minutes
total). Divide dough in half. Cover
and let rest for 10 minutes.

▌▌ On the floured surface, roll *each*
portion of dough to ⅜-inch
thickness for large dogs or ¼-inch
thickness for small dogs. Using 2-
to 4-inch cutters, cut dough into
desired shapes. Place shapes on
ungreased baking sheets.

▌▌ Brush tops with a mixture of the
egg and milk. Bake in a 300° oven
for 35 minutes for the ¼-inch-thick
biscuits or 45 minutes for the ⅜-
inch-thick biscuits. Turn oven off.
Let biscuits dry overnight in oven
with door closed. Makes 24 to 30
biscuits.

Homemade Dog Snacks: Prepare
and roll out dough as directed at
left, *except do not cut dough.* Brush top
with the mixture of egg and milk.
Using a pastry wheel, cut dough
into ½-inch-wide strips, then cut
the strips crosswise into ½-inch
pieces. *Or,* using 1-inch cutters, cut
dough into desired shapes. Using a
wide spatula, transfer pieces to
ungreased baking sheets. Bake in a
300° oven for 30 minutes, then dry
as directed at left. Makes about 30
dozen (9 cups) of the ½-inch
pieces.

*T*o **store:** Prepare
Homemade Dog Biscuits or
Homemade Dog Snacks as
directed above. Transfer
biscuits or snacks to a plastic
bag or container. Seal, label,
and place in a cool, dry place
for up to 3 months.

Ode to Saint Nicholas! In the Netherlands, each year little boys and girls leave their wooden shoes by the chimney on the eve of December 5 in hopes that Saint Nicholas will ride by on his horse and fill their shoes with goodies.

This holiday season, bring this tradition closer to home. Begin the same custom with family and friends by giving them wooden shoes stuffed with mixed nuts and candy-coated milk chocolate pieces. Then, year after year, the shoes can be set out again with anticipation of having them replenished with goodies.

'Tis the seasoning! Nothing's better on a cold winter's night than a cup of spiced cider or a bowl of spicy chili. Warm up a friend or neighbor with a gift of a special recipe and some spices. Simply choose one of your favorite spicy recipes and copy it on a recipe card. Then, package up the spices used in the recipe and deliver your package with love.

Holiday Fun

FOR KIDS TO CRAFT

"It is good to be children sometimes and never better than at Christmas, when its Mighty Founder was a child himself."

Charles Dickens

When cold and wet keep children indoors, turn their hands and minds to the happy diversion of making their own gifts and treats. Designed just for children, these easy-to-do ornaments and favors require little adult supervision, so children can take pride in a gift they've made all by themselves. What better way to teach a child that Christmas comes from the heart, not from the store?

Candy-Filled Vinyl Tubing Wreath

Take a trip to the hardware store to find materials for this fun-filled ornament. Pour colorful little candies into the tubing, then shape the wreath. Decorated with artificial greens and berries, this easy-to-make wreath can be hung on your tree or given as a gift.

MATERIALS

For one ornament

12 inches of ⅜-inch-diameter vinyl tubing

⅜-inch-diameter wooden peg

Tiny candies

Sprigs of artificial greenery and berries

Two strips of 4-inch-long florist's wire

12 inches of ½-inch-wide red satin ribbon

10 inches of red string

INSTRUCTIONS

1 Fill the tube with candies. Join the ends of the tube with the wooden peg. Position the peg at the top of the wreath.

2 Fold the red string in half and loop it around the top of the wreath. Knot the ends of the string to make a loop for hanging.

3 Crisscross two pieces of artificial greenery at the top of the wreath. Secure the greens to the wreath by wrapping and twisting florist wire around both the greens and the wreath. In the same way, add two sprigs of berries over the greens.

4 Tie a ribbon bow around the top of the wreath. Trim the ribbon ends.

Bird's Nest Ornament

Throughout the cold and wintry days, your backyard bird friends will welcome these hearty treats.

MATERIALS

For one ornament

Purchased 3-inch-diameter bird nest with wire hangers (available at craft stores)

Peanut butter

Sunflower seeds and other birdseed

Butter knife

Paper plate

12 inches of ½-inch-wide ribbon

INSTRUCTIONS

1 With the butter knife, spread peanut butter around the sides of the nest.

2 Pour some birdseed onto the paper plate. Roll the sides of the nest on the plate so the birdseed sticks to the peanut butter. Use your fingers to push sunflower seeds into the peanut butter.

3 Tie the ribbon into a bow at the bottom of the nest around the wire hangers. Fasten the nest to your tree, using the wires to secure it to the branches.

Candy Bar Race Cars

Take to the tracks with a completely edible Christmas treat! These little race cars and sleds make fun party favors. Just use cake frosting instead of glue to stick peppermints or candy canes onto miniature candy bars.

MATERIALS

Chocolate-covered candy bars
Striped peppermint candies
  for wheels
Round candy-coated
  chocolate pieces for
  steering wheels
Tube or can of cake frosting
Butter knife

INSTRUCTIONS

1 To make the driver's seat in each race car, use the butter knife to scoop out a shallow, ½-inch-wide wedge across the center of each candy bar.

2 Use a dab of frosting to fasten a small candy on the driver's side of the wedge for a steering wheel. Use frosting to stick peppermint candies on the sides for the wheels. Refrigerate the cars to set the frosting.

Candy Bar Sleds

MATERIALS
Small candy canes
Chocolate-covered candy bars
Mellowcreme toy candies
Tube or can of cake frosting

INSTRUCTIONS

1 Cut off ¼ inch of the curved tip on each of two candy canes. Use cake frosting to stick the canes to the bottom of the candy bar to make sled runners.

2 Use frosting to fasten toy candies to the top of the sled. Don't handle the sleds until the frosting is set.

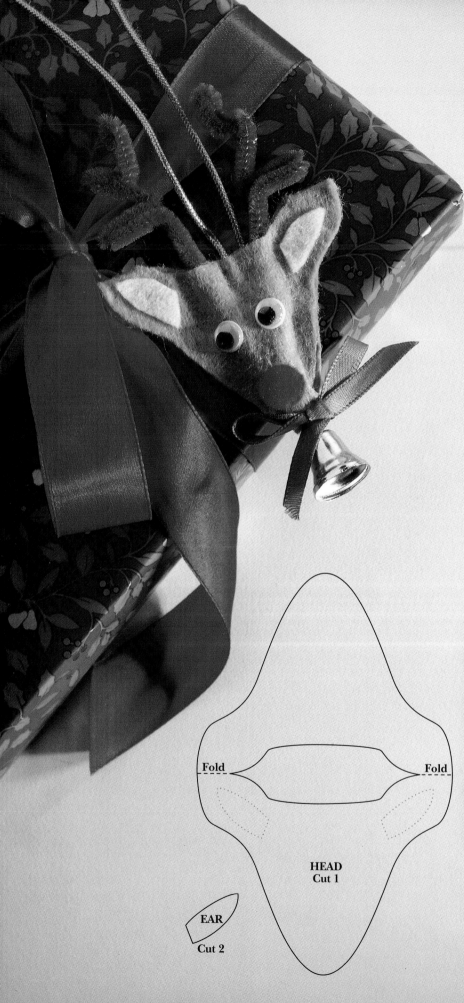

Reindeer Necklace

Holiday jewelry is fun to make and wear. Our reindeer pal is a fast and easy trinket to make for keeps or as a gift. Use a shorter cord to make a tree ornament.

MATERIALS

Tan and pink felt scraps
Brown pipe cleaner
16 mm gold-tone bell
1¼-inch-diameter pom-pom
30 inches of gold cord
10 inches of ¼-inch-wide
  green satin ribbon
Two 8 mm moving eyes
Tacky glue; scissors
Tracing paper and pencil

INSTRUCTIONS

1 Trace the head and ear patterns, *left,* onto tracing paper. Using paper patterns, cut the head from tan felt and the ears from pink felt.

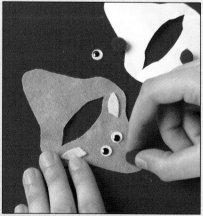

2 Glue the felt ears, moving eyes, and the pom-pom nose onto one side of the reindeer's head.

Fold   Fold

HEAD
Cut 1

EAR

Cut 2

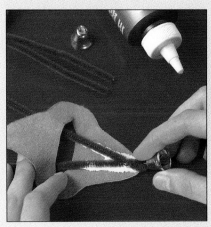

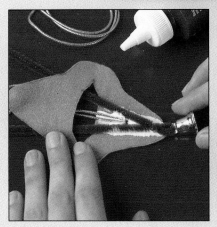

3 Slip the pipe cleaner through the hanger at the top of the bell. Bend the pipe cleaner in half with the bell at the fold. Twist both strands together just above the bell. Working with the wrong side of the head piece faceup, push the pipe cleaner ends through the center opening in the head. Glue the pipe cleaner to one side of the head, letting the twist in the pipe cleaner and the bell dangle below the chin.

4 Glue the ends of the cord between the strands of the pipe cleaner. Take the loop of the cord through the center opening in the head piece.

5 On the wrong side, run a thin band of glue around the edges of the bottom head piece. Fold the top head piece over and glue the two heads together. Bend the pipe cleaner ends into the shape of antlers.

6 Tie the green ribbon into a bow. Glue the bow knot over the twist of the pipe cleaner below the chin. Trim the ribbon ends.

Feathered Friend Ornament

Dressed in festive colors, a flock of fantasy birds will proudly display your handiwork on this year's Christmas tree.

MATERIALS
For one ornament

One 1½-inch-diameter plastic foam ball for the body

One 1-inch-diameter plastic foam ball for the head

Feathers in assorted colors

Two 5 mm pom-poms for the eyes

Scrap of construction paper for the beak

Two colors of glitter

Scissors

Tacky glue; waxed paper

Paper plate; toothpicks

One small wooden clothespin

INSTRUCTIONS

1 Insert a toothpick into the larger plastic foam ball. Holding the toothpick, squeeze glue onto the ball. Use another toothpick to spread the glue evenly over the surface of the ball.

2 Working over the paper plate, sprinkle glitter over the ball until it is completely covered. Remove the toothpick. Set the ball on waxed paper to dry.

3 Repeat steps 1 and 2 to cover the second ball with the other color of glitter. Do not remove the toothpick from the second ball.

5 Using the pattern, *above*, cut out a paper beak. Crease the beak along the fold lines and overlap the folded tabs to shape it. Dab glue on the tabs and glue the beak onto the head. Glue on the pom-pom eyes.

4 Break off the end of the toothpick so that ½ inch remains. Dab glue on the broken end and push it into the large ball to join the bird's head and body pieces.

6 Press a clothespin into the base of the body to slightly indent the foam. Dab glue over the indentation and glue the clothespin in place. Let the glue dry.

7 Using assorted colors, push five feathers into the back of the bird to make a tail. Insert three feathers in each side of the body to make the wings.

Roly-Poly Santa Ornament

These jolly ornaments are made from blown-out eggs and lots of punched paper dots. The twinkling moving eyes are available in a variety of colors at crafts stores.

MATERIALS

For one ornament
One egg
8-inch length of gold cord for the hanger
Red, pink, white, black, and yellow construction paper
Paper punch; scissors
Tacky glue
Toothpick; straight pin
Tracing paper and pencil
Two 4 mm movable eyes

INSTRUCTIONS

1 Wash the egg in warm, soapy water; rinse and dry. Referring to the diagram, *below, left,* use the straight pin to poke a small hole in the top and bottom of the egg. Holding the egg over a bowl, place your mouth over one hole and blow hard. The egg contents will come out the other hole. Rinse the egg and set it aside to dry.

2 Glue the ends of the cord into the hole at the narrow end of the egg, enlarging the hole as necessary.

3 Paper-punch a lot of dots from a piece of folded red construction paper.

4 Squeeze a dab of glue onto the narrow end of the egg and spread it around with the toothpick. Fasten red dots on the glued area. *Do not cover the hole.* Continue adding glue and fastening dots until the egg is covered. Set the egg aside to let the glue dry.

5 Trace the patterns at *left* and *opposite* onto tracing paper. Using the tracing paper patterns, cut each shape from construction paper.

MUSTACHE

FACE

BEARD

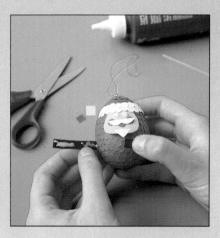

6 Glue three red dots onto the face for the mouth and cheeks. Glue on the beard and mustache. Glue the top edge of the face piece about ¾ inch from the top of the narrow part of the egg. Let the glue dry.

7 Punch dots from white construction paper. Glue two rows of white dots around the egg so they overlap the top edge of the face. Glue the two moving eyes onto the face piece.

8 Glue a black belt around the egg just below Santa's chin and underneath his beard. Glue the small black rectangle atop the yellow buckle, then glue the buckle to the center front of the belt.

Yellow

Black

→ Black (Cut to length that fits around egg)

BELT

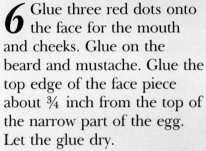

Elf Finger Puppets

Quick as a wink, you can make finger-puppet elves from an old rubber glove, scraps of felt, and a rubber band. Then stage a puppet show that tells the story of how the elves are busy helping Santa prepare for his Christmas Eve travels.

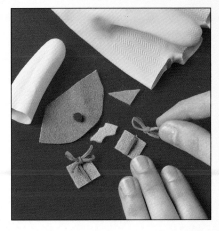

MATERIALS
Rubber glove
Tracing paper and pencil
Scraps of felt
Scissors
Small red pom-poms
Rubber band
Tacky glue
Black felt-tip pen

INSTRUCTIONS

1 Cut one finger off the rubber glove. Turn the finger wrong side out.

2 Trace the patterns, *right,* onto tracing paper and cut out the paper patterns. Using the photos as a guide for colors, cut each piece from scraps of felt.

3 Cut a strip of rubber band to fit the length of the package and glue it in place on the felt. Tie the remaining piece of rubber band into a bow and glue the bow to the top of the package. Set the package aside to let the glue dry.

4 Glue the straight edges of the hat together, making a cone shape. Glue the hat to the tip of the cut-off glove finger. With the glued edge of the hat facing the back, glue a holly leaf and a pom-pom berry to the front of the hat. Glue the hair under the front edge of the hat.

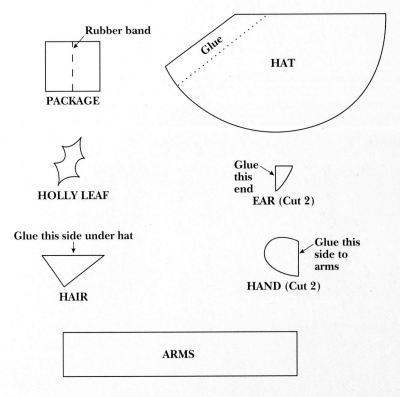

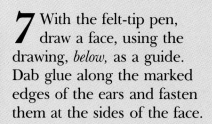

7 With the felt-tip pen, draw a face, using the drawing, *below,* as a guide. Dab glue along the marked edges of the ears and fasten them at the sides of the face.

5 Glue the assembled package onto the glove finger about 1 inch under the front rim of the hat.

6 Glue a hand to each end of the arms piece. Glue the center of the arm piece on the back of the puppet about ½ inch below the hat. Dab glue on the hands and fasten them onto the package.

Sponge Ornaments

Transform ordinary kitchen sponges into glitzy, cheery holiday ornaments using cookie cutters to outline the holiday shapes. Beads, sequins, paint, and a drop of glue are all you need!

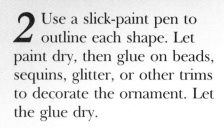

MATERIALS
Colored sponges
Felt-tip pen
Cookie cutters
Slick-paint pens
Beads, sequins, glitter, and
    other trims
Scissors
Crafts glue
Gold cord or thread for
    hanging loops
Sewing needle

INSTRUCTIONS

1 Prepare the sponges by soaking them for a few minutes in plain warm water. Let the sponges dry before making the ornaments.

Using the felt-tip pen, draw an ornament design onto the sponge. Or, trace a shape around a cookie cutter. Cut out the drawn shape.

2 Use a slick-paint pen to outline each shape. Let paint dry, then glue on beads, sequins, glitter, or other trims to decorate the ornament. Let the glue dry.

3 Thread the needle with gold cord or thread. Push the needle through the top of the ornament. Remove the needle. Knot the ends of the cord together to make a loop for hanging.

Greatest Gifts
MADE WITH LOVE

"The only real blind person at Christmastime is he who has not Christmas in his heart." Helen Keller, 1906

If it sometimes seems that gift-giving is getting out of hand, remind yourself that the spirit of the gift—not its price tag—is what's really important. Does anything say "I love you" like a gift you made yourself? Let these ideas prompt you to give homemade gifts this season. In years to come, these decorative accessories will become all the more loved, forever cherished as reminders of you and this year's Christmas at home.

Mr. & Mrs. Fisher Cat Dolls

Cats are approximately 10 inches tall.

MATERIALS
¼ yard *each* of muslin and black solid fabric
9x18 inches of print fabric for dress
5x14 inches of plaid apron fabric
9-inch square fabric for shirt
¼ yard of narrow black cording
Acrylic paints in ginger-brown, black, and light tan; paintbrush
Polyester filling
Black embroidery floss
Black quilting or carpet thread
5-inch-long twig and scrap of string for fishing pole
Tracing paper or template material
Fabric marker or pencil

INSTRUCTIONS
Making the cat dolls
Trace the cat body patterns, *opposite,* and the tail pattern on page 119 onto tracing paper or clear template material. Mark grain lines on all pieces. Cut out a paper or plastic template for each pattern. These patterns include a ¼-inch-wide seam allowance.

Trace around each template on the *wrong* side of each fabric, positioning the template grain line parallel to the selvage. For *each* cat, cut the number of each piece indicated on the pattern. Cut body pieces for one cat from black fabric and body pieces for the other cat from the muslin.

BODY: Sew front and back body pieces together, leaving the bottom edges open. Join two pairs of arms, legs, and ears of the same fabric. Stitch tail pieces together. Clip seam allowances; turn all pieces right side out. Stuff the body, arms, and legs through openings.

Center legs in the body opening, spaced ¼ inch apart. Fold opening edges under ¼ inch and topstitch, catching legs in the stitching.

Fold opening edges under ¼ inch at the top of each arm and hand-sew arms to shoulders. Stitch ears to the head in the same manner, pinching a small pleat in the bottom of each ear as you sew.

Do not attach tail yet. Make both cats in this same manner.

PAINTING: For the muslin cat, paint the head, arms, feet, and tail with two coats of ginger-brown paint. Paint

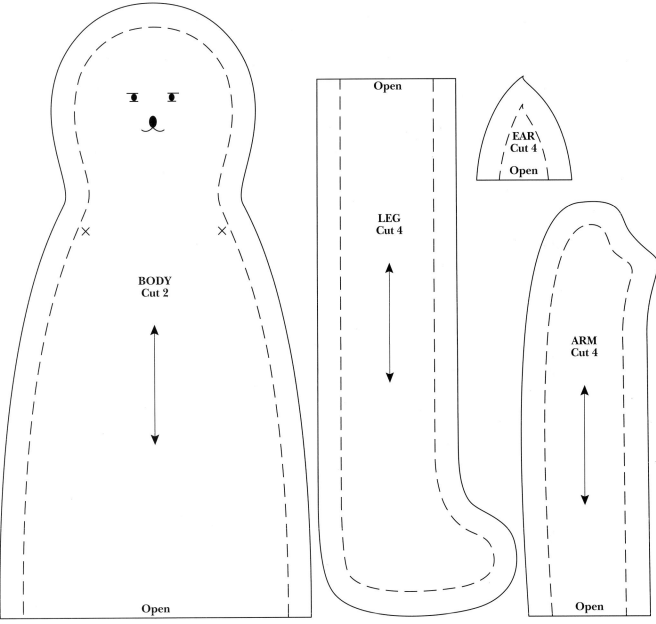

MR. AND MRS. FISHER CAT DOLLS PATTERNS

the tail tip black. It is not necessary to paint the parts of the body that will be covered by clothing.

On the black cat, paint the tip of the tail and a ¾-inch-wide stripe on the face with light tan paint.

On each cat's face, draw small eyes, a nose, and a mouth with black paint. Add tiger stripes, if desired. Let all paint dry completely before adding clothes.

WHISKERS: Thread three strands of quilting thread onto the needle and make a knot 1½ inches from the end of the thread. Insert the needle on one side of the nose and bring it out on the other side. Pull thread taut to bring knot against the fabric. Knot the thread on the other side close to the nose; clip thread 1½ inches from the knot.

Making the dolls' clothing
Make paper or plastic templates for the clothing patterns on pages 118 and 119. Cut the number of pieces indicated on each pattern. Cut Mr. Cat's pants from scraps of black fabric. For Mrs. Cat's bloomers, cut two 4½x6¾-inch rectangles from the remaining muslin.

SHIRT: With right sides together, join shirt pieces at the shoulder seam, stitching from sleeve edge to the dot on each side. Press seam allowances open, including neck opening. Sew underarm/side seams. Turn shirt to right side and slip it onto the doll.

Tuck a small pleat in the shirt front. Use floss to make small horizontal stitches through all layers to tack the pleat in place. If the shirt does not fit snugly at the neck, stitch a little tuck at each shoulder seam.

continued

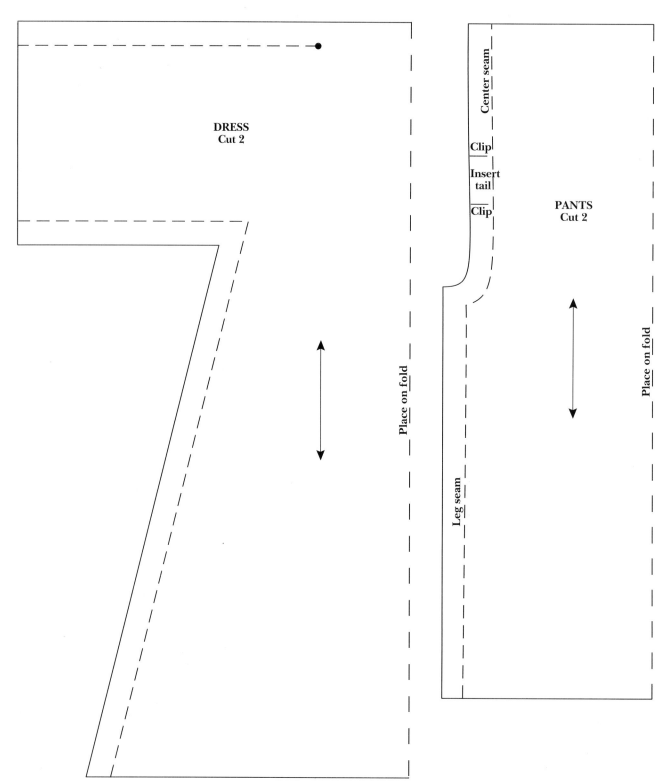

DRESS
Cut 2

Place on fold

Center seam

Clip

Insert tail

Clip

PANTS
Cut 2

Place on fold

Leg seam

MR. AND MRS. FISHER CAT DOLLS PATTERNS

Turn under a ¼-inch hem at the bottom of each sleeve. Gather sleeve bottom to fit snugly around the arm.

PANTS: Join pants pieces at center front seam. Stitch the center back seam, sewing the tail into the seam as indicated on the pattern. Stitch the inner leg seam.

Turn under a ¼-inch hem at the bottom of each leg and at the waist. Pull pants onto the doll. Gather waist and pant legs to fit. Knot the cording tight around the waist for a belt.

Tie a knot in one end of the string; tie the other end around the twig. Push the twig through the belt and Mr. Cat is ready to go a-fishin'.

BLOOMERS: On each muslin rectangle, find the center of one short side. From this center point, measure and mark a vertical line 4¼ inches long into the center of the fabric. Cut the fabric on this line.

Stitch the two rectangles together, right sides together, along the long sides, then sew the inner seams. Turn bloomers right side out.

Press under a ¼-inch hem at the bottom of each leg and at the waist. Pull bloomers onto the doll, then gather legs and waist to fit.

DRESS AND APRON: Make dress in same manner as for shirt. Topstitch a ¼-inch hem at the bottom before slipping dress onto the doll.

From plaid fabric, cut a 3¾x13-inch rectangle for the apron and a 1x6½-inch strip for the waistband.

Sew short ends of apron piece together, sewing the tail into the seam about ¾ inch from the top edge. Topstitch a hem at the bottom.

With right sides together, fold the waistband in half lengthwise; stitch short ends together. Turn waistband right side out. Gather top edge of apron to fit the waistband. Matching back seams and raw edges, stitch waistband to apron. Turn waistband over seam allowance and topstitch.

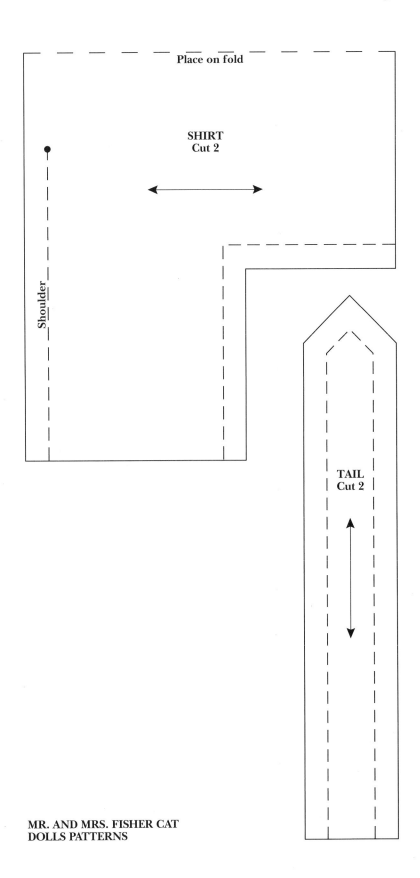

MR. AND MRS. FISHER CAT DOLLS PATTERNS

Noel Cross-Stitch

*Finished stitchery is approximately
5 inches square. Stitch count is
70 stitches square.*

MATERIALS

One 12-inch square of 14-count
   oatmeal-colored Aida cloth
One skein of floss in each color
   listed on color key, *below*
4 inches of ⅛-inch-wide red satin
   ribbon
Tapestry needle
Embroidery hoop
Graph paper, pencil, and ruler

INSTRUCTIONS

Referring to the chart, *below*, work
cross-stitches over one square of the
Aida cloth with three strands of floss.
Center the design on the fabric.

   When cross-stitching is complete,
work backstitches with one strand of
floss. Use the letters in the alphabet

chart, *below*, to work out a name or
message on graph paper. Center and
backstitch the message in the space
provided, using two strands of floss.

   Tie the ribbon into a small bow;
tack the bow in place below the birdhouse door. Press the finished stitchery. Frame as desired.

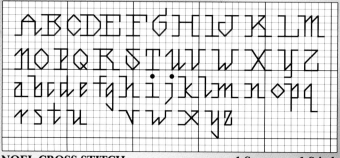

NOEL CROSS-STITCH   1 Square = 1 Stitch

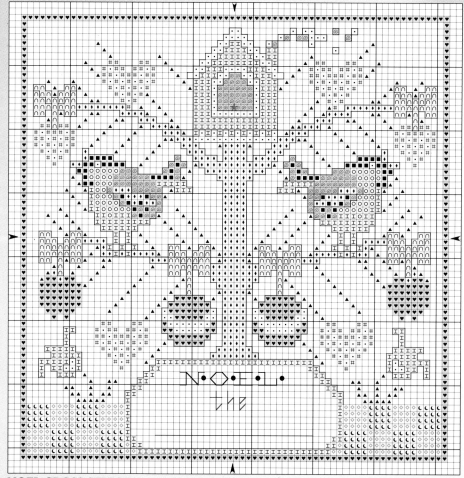

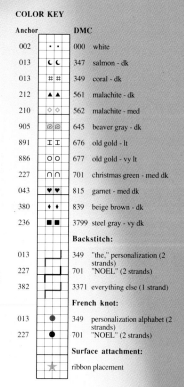

COLOR KEY

Anchor		DMC	
002	··	000	white
013	CC	347	salmon - dk
013	##	349	coral - dk
212	▲▲	561	malachite - dk
210	◇◇	562	malachite - med
905	⊚⊚	645	beaver gray - dk
891	II	676	old gold - lt
886	○○	677	old gold - vy lt
227	∩∩	701	christmas green - med dk
043	♥♥	815	garnet - med dk
380	♦♦	839	beige brown - dk
236	■■	3799	steel gray - vy dk

Backstitch:

013		349	"the," personalization (2 strands)
227		701	"NOEL" (2 strands)
382		3371	everything else (1 strand)

French knot:

013	●	349	personalization alphabet (2 strands)
227	●	701	"NOEL" (2 strands)

Surface attachment:

	★	ribbon placement

Fabrics and finished design sizes:

11 Aida, 6-3/8"h x 6-3/8"w
14 Aida, 5"h x 5"w
18 Aida, 3-7/8"h x 3-7/8"w
22 Hardanger, 3-1/4"h x 3-1/4"w

NOEL CROSS-STITCH   1 Square = 1 Stitch

Bernice and Barney Bunny Dolls

Each bunny is 12 inches tall.

MATERIALS
For two dolls
½ yard of imitation fur for body
5x9-inch piece of ear lining fabric
8x22-inch piece of ticking for
  overalls and bag
4x7-inch piece of osnaburg, burlap,
  or muslin for seed bag
Two 9x11-inch rectangles of cotton
  fabric for Bernice's dress
⅝ yard of 1-inch-wide flat lace
14 inches *each* of narrow string for
  bags and jute for suspenders
Four 7-mm brown sew-on eyes with
  safety locks
Polyester fiberfill
Black embroidery floss
Black carpet thread for whiskers
Tracing paper or template material
Permanent fabric marker

INSTRUCTIONS
Cutting the body fabric
Trace the bunny body patterns, *opposite* and on pages 124 and 125, onto tracing paper or translucent template material. Include grain lines on each tracing. Make one tracing for the back, joining the two parts of the pattern on the dotted lines as indicated. Cut out a paper or plastic template for each piece. These patterns include a ⅛-inch-wide seam allowance.

Trace around each template on the *wrong* side of the fur, placing the grain line parallel to the direction of the pile (the smoothed pile should run *down* on all pieces). Mark and cut one layer at a time; be sure to flip the templates for the head front and body front over to mark the second piece required. Cut the number of each piece indicated on the pattern for *each* bunny.

Making the bunny body
Note: Keep long strands of fur away from the stitching as much as possible. If some fur gets caught in the stitching, slip a pin under the trapped strands and gently pick them out of the seam. Brush fur over the seam to camouflage it.

BODY: With right sides together, sew a foot to the bottom edge of each front body piece. Stitch front body pieces together from neck to notch.

With right sides together, sew the front to the back, stitching from one side of the neck opening around to the other. Leave neck open. Clip curves; turn body right side out.

Push stuffing down into the feet. Bend feet at the body/foot seam line and tack in place, hiding the tacking stitches in the pile of the fur. Stuff remainder of body firmly.

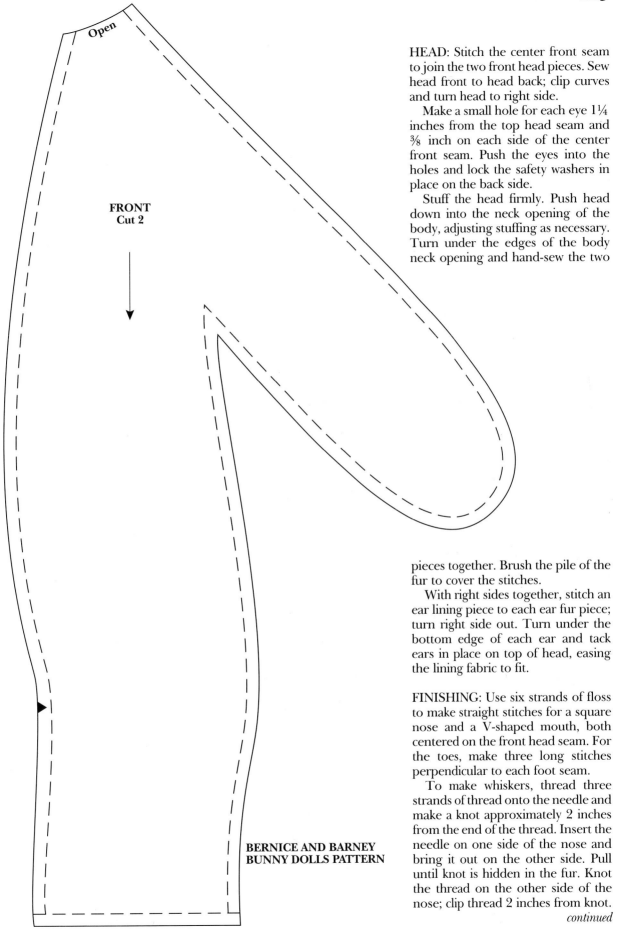

Open

FRONT
Cut 2

BERNICE AND BARNEY
BUNNY DOLLS PATTERN

HEAD: Stitch the center front seam to join the two front head pieces. Sew head front to head back; clip curves and turn head to right side.

Make a small hole for each eye 1¼ inches from the top head seam and ⅜ inch on each side of the center front seam. Push the eyes into the holes and lock the safety washers in place on the back side.

Stuff the head firmly. Push head down into the neck opening of the body, adjusting stuffing as necessary. Turn under the edges of the body neck opening and hand-sew the two pieces together. Brush the pile of the fur to cover the stitches.

With right sides together, stitch an ear lining piece to each ear fur piece; turn right side out. Turn under the bottom edge of each ear and tack ears in place on top of head, easing the lining fabric to fit.

FINISHING: Use six strands of floss to make straight stitches for a square nose and a V-shaped mouth, both centered on the front head seam. For the toes, make three long stitches perpendicular to each foot seam.

To make whiskers, thread three strands of thread onto the needle and make a knot approximately 2 inches from the end of the thread. Insert the needle on one side of the nose and bring it out on the other side. Pull until knot is hidden in the fur. Knot the thread on the other side of the nose; clip thread 2 inches from knot.

continued

Making the bunny clothes

Before cutting fabrics and lace for the bunnies' clothing and bags, see page 157 for tips on tea-dyeing. Dry and press tea-dyed fabrics before cutting.

Make a paper or plastic template for the overalls pattern, *opposite*, and the dress pattern on page 126. Cut two of each pattern from the appropriate fabric. These patterns include a ¼-inch-wide seam allowance. For the overalls bib, cut one 3x2½-inch piece of ticking.

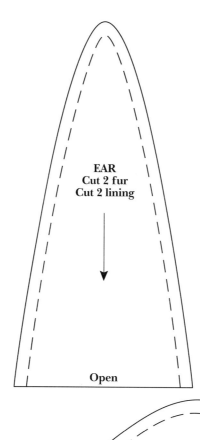

EAR
Cut 2 fur
Cut 2 lining

Open

FOOT
CUT 2

Open

BACK
Cut 1

Join back pattern on dotted line

Place on fold

OVERALLS: With right sides together, stitch center front and back seams of overalls. Sew the inner leg seam; clip curves and turn overalls right side out. Turn under a ¼-inch hem on each leg and around three sides of the bib piece; topstitch.

Press under a ½-inch hem around the top edge of the pants. Pin bib in place at center front, then topstitch around the pants' edge.

Pull overalls onto the bunny. Tack one end of a 7-inch piece of jute to each top corner of the bib; turn the jute over to the back, crossing the strands in the middle of the back. Tack the other ends to the pants' back. Adjust jute length if necessary.

continued

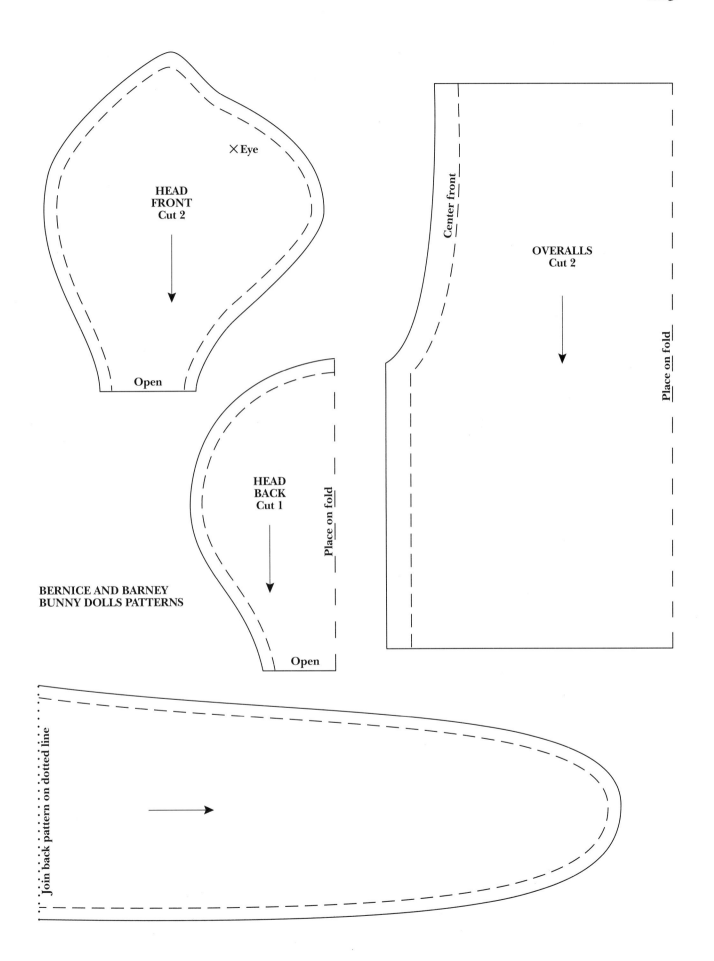

×Eye

**HEAD
FRONT
Cut 2**

Open

**OVERALLS
Cut 2**

Center front

Place on fold

**HEAD
BACK
Cut 1**

Place on fold

Open

**BERNICE AND BARNEY
BUNNY DOLLS PATTERNS**

Join back pattern on dotted line

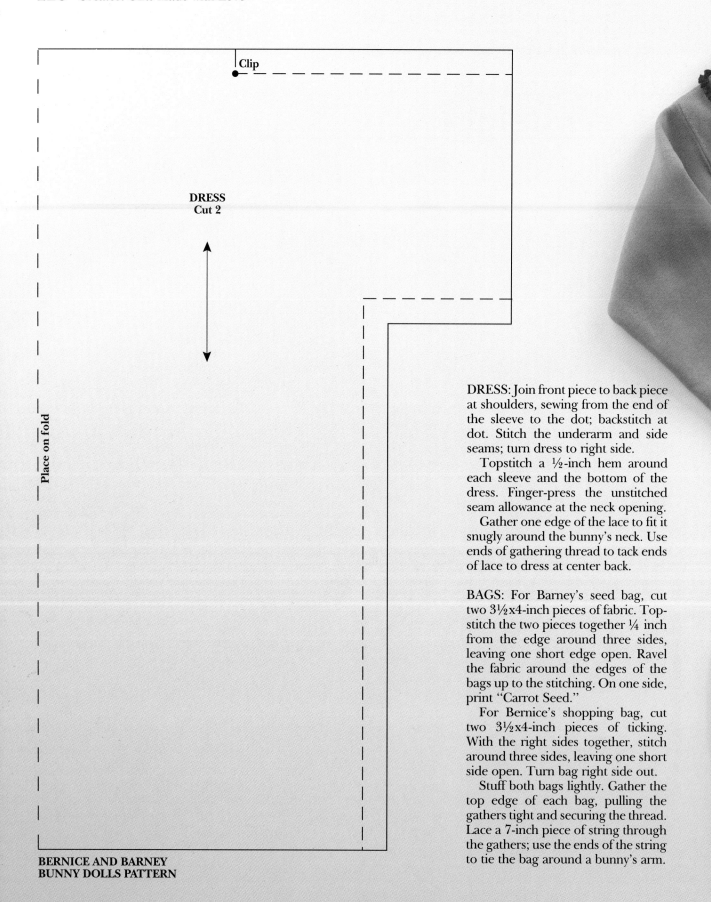

Clip

DRESS
Cut 2

Place on fold

BERNICE AND BARNEY
BUNNY DOLLS PATTERN

DRESS: Join front piece to back piece at shoulders, sewing from the end of the sleeve to the dot; backstitch at dot. Stitch the underarm and side seams; turn dress to right side.

Topstitch a ½-inch hem around each sleeve and the bottom of the dress. Finger-press the unstitched seam allowance at the neck opening.

Gather one edge of the lace to fit it snugly around the bunny's neck. Use ends of gathering thread to tack ends of lace to dress at center back.

BAGS: For Barney's seed bag, cut two 3½x4-inch pieces of fabric. Topstitch the two pieces together ¼ inch from the edge around three sides, leaving one short edge open. Ravel the fabric around the edges of the bags up to the stitching. On one side, print "Carrot Seed."

For Bernice's shopping bag, cut two 3½x4-inch pieces of ticking. With the right sides together, stitch around three sides, leaving one short side open. Turn bag right side out.

Stuff both bags lightly. Gather the top edge of each bag, pulling the gathers tight and securing the thread. Lace a 7-inch piece of string through the gathers; use the ends of the string to tie the bag around a bunny's arm.

Child's Embellished Sweatshirt

MATERIALS

Purchased sweatshirt
Gloves or mittens
Decorative trims such as fabric
  paint, rickrack, ribbon, buttons,
  beads, and rhinestones

INSTRUCTIONS

Position gloves or mittens on the shirt at an angle the child will find comfortable for pockets. Whipstitch around each glove or mitten, leaving the cuff open. Add decorative embellishments as desired.

Tiny Teddy Bear

Bear is approximately 4½ inches tall.

MATERIALS
⅛ yard of cotton or wool fabric or imitation fur
Scraps of contrasting fabric for feet
14 inches of ¼-inch-wide ribbon or ½-inch-wide strip of contrasting wool fabric for muffler
Two 5-mm black beads for eyes
Black embroidery floss for nose
Carpet thread; doll sculpture needle
Polyester fiberfill
Plastic pellets for filling (optional)
Tracing paper or template material
Fine-tipped fabric marker

INSTRUCTIONS
Cutting the fabric
Trace the bear patterns, *opposite,* onto tracing paper or translucent template material. These patterns include a ⅛-inch-wide seam allowance. Make a template for each pattern piece. Mark all dots, opening notches, and grain lines on each template.

Trace around each template on the *wrong* side of the bear fabric, placing the template grain line parallel to the grain of the fabric or nap of the fur. Cut the number of each piece indicated on each pattern. *Note:* If using imitation fur, mark and cut one layer at a time; be sure to flip the template over so half of the required pieces are reversed.

Use a pin or scrap of thread to mark dots on the right sides of the body, arm, and leg pieces.

Making the bear's body
Note: Keep long strands of fur away from the stitching as much as possible. If some fur gets caught in the stitching, slip a pin under the trapped strands and gently pick them out of the seam. Brush fur over the seam to camouflage it.

BODY: With right sides together, join the two body pieces; leave top edge open as indicated. Turn body right side out.

Fill the bottom half of the body with plastic pellets, topped with a small amount of polyester fiberfill to soften the body. Or, for a lighter and softer bear, use fiberfill only.

HEAD: With wrong sides together, join the two head pieces from the tip of the nose down to the front of the neck as illustrated in Figure 1, *right.*

Align the center of the nose gusset with this front seam as shown in Figure 2, *far right.* Working from center front to the back neck, hand-stitch the gusset to one side of the head. Stitch gusset to other head piece, again working from front to back.

Turn head right side out and stuff firmly with polyester fiberfill.

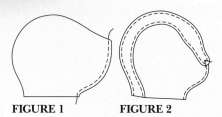

FIGURE 1   **FIGURE 2**

Using a strong carpet thread, hand-sew a gathering stitch around the top opening of the body and the bottom opening of the head. Gather both edges slightly, but do not pull the edges tightly together.

Aligning center front seams and adjusting the gathered edges to fit, hand-stitch head to body, using the carpet thread. Stitch around the seam several times to secure.

ARMS: Sew two arm pieces together, leaving an opening as indicated on the pattern. Turn arm right side out; stuff with pellets or polyester fiberfill. Blindstitch the opening closed. Make another arm in the same manner.

Matching dots, sew arms onto the body using a long sculpture needle and carpet thread. Insert the needle into one arm, through the body, and out the other arm. Pull the thread tight; reinsert the needle and repeat in the other direction. Try to push the needle through the same spot each time to keep the arms moveable.

LEGS: Sew two leg pieces together, leaving openings at one side and at the bottom straight edge as indicated on the pattern. Matching the centers of each foot pad with the leg seams, sew a foot pad to the bottom edge of each leg; ease leg opening to fit foot pad as necessary. Make another leg in the same manner.

Turn legs right side out through openings. (It may be difficult to turn fur through the small openings, but careful manipulation will do the job.) Fill leg with pellets or polyester fiberfill; blindstitch the openings closed.

Join legs to the body in the same manner as you did the arms.

EARS: Sew two ear pieces together, leaving the bottom edge open. Turn ear right side out. Repeat for the other ear. Turn under the seam allowance at the bottom of each ear and hand-sew ears to head. Center each ear over the gusset seam.

FINISHING: Using a long piece of six-strand embroidery floss, sew bead eyes in place atop the gusset seam. Pull the thread tight to indent the fabric slightly. Before knotting off the thread, embroider straight stitches at the tip of the gusset seam for a nose.

Tie a ribbon bow around the neck. Or knot a wool fabric scrap around the neck and ravel the edges.

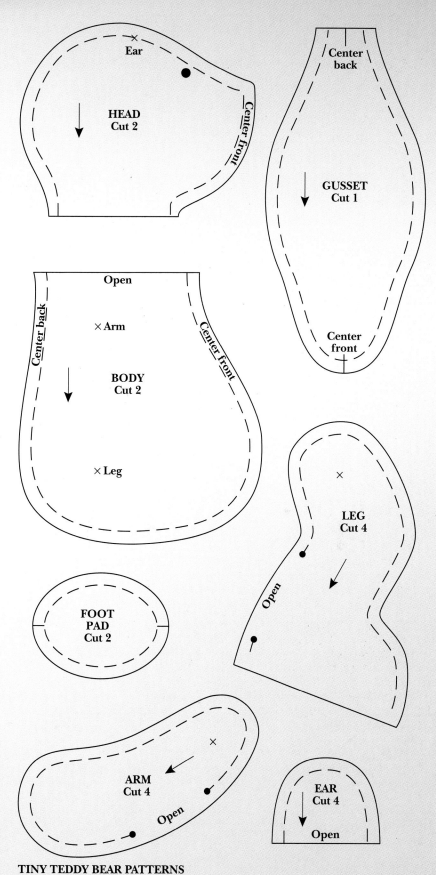

TINY TEDDY BEAR PATTERNS

Merry Christmas

Queen Anne's Lace Snowflake Note Card

Folded card measures 3¾x5½ inches.

MATERIALS

5½x7½-inch piece of colored construction paper or 70-pound
writing paper with a deckle edge
(a torn look often used in fine
stationery), available at stationery
and printing shops
4x6-inch matching envelope
Four Queen Anne's lace flowers
5x7-inch piece of white bond paper
to use with construction paper
(optional)
Glue stick; white crafts glue
White or clear glitter
Toothpicks; butter knife
Scissors; sewing needle

INSTRUCTIONS

Pressed Queen Anne's lace turns
memories of summer's magic into a
sparkling wintertime thank-you note
or greeting card.

If you are working with construction paper, you may want to glue
white bond to one side to have a nice
writing surface. Apply glue around
the edges of the bond. (Putting glue
in the middle makes the paper ripple
when the glue dries. Center the bond
on the construction paper, leaving a
¼-inch margin of colored paper on
all sides.

Collecting and drying the flowers

Queen Anne's lace, or wild carrot,
grows wild almost everywhere in the
United States from late June through
early autumn. Pick flowers on a dry
day after the morning dew burns off,
since moist flowers may get moldy
when pressed. Collect four flowers in
a variety of sizes for each card.

Remove the stem from each flower. Lay the flowers in a single layer
between sheets of newspaper; place
the paper under heavy books or
bricks. Let the "press" stand for approximately one week or until the
flowers are completely dry.

Many Queen Anne's lace flowers
have a tiny purple center. You can
leave these in place or, if you want all-
white flowers, gently prick them out
of the dried flowers with the point of
a sewing needle. Handle the delicate
dried flowers with care.

Decorating the card

Fold the notepaper in half to measure 3¾x5½ inches. If working with
construction paper, fold the white
bond paper to the inside.

Arrange the dried flowers on the
front of the card as desired. Use a
toothpick to apply little dabs of white
glue to the back of each flower. Slide
a butter knife under the flower to lift
it and turn it over so the glued side is
against the card; let glue dry.

Drip little spots of glue onto the
tips and center of each flower, as well
as randomly on the background paper. Pour glitter over the card, wait a
minute, then shake off excess glitter.

For an extra touch, add a flower to
one inside corner of the card.

Holiday Puzzles

MATERIALS

Greeting card, wrapping paper, or
  other printed picture (we used
  cards, stickers, and gift bags by
  The Gifted Line, 999 Canal
  Blvd., Port Richmond, CA 94804;
  1-800-5-GIFTED)
$5/4$ or 1-inch clear redwood, slightly
  larger than image area
All-purpose tacky glue
$\frac{1}{2}$ pound of paste finishing wax
  mixed with 3 tablespoons of
  burnt umber oil paint
Small paintbrush
Scraps of twine or rug yarn
Scissors or crafts knife
Satin spray varnish
Scroll saw; belt sander

INSTRUCTIONS

Cut desired image from the paper
product. Apply glue to back of paper;
fasten paper to the wood block,
smoothing out all wrinkles and air
bubbles. Let glue dry overnight. *Note:*
Put a brick or sheet of glass on top of
the wood block while the paper dries.

For an antiqued look, brush a thin
layer of diluted finishing wax over the
surface; let dry. Apply spray varnish.

Cut wood to match the paper outline; sand edges smooth. Cut puzzle
pieces as desired, making each one
different. Be sure pieces interlock so
the puzzle will hold together.

Tie a scrap of twine or rug yarn
tight around the puzzle to hold it together for gift-giving.

Keepsake Albums

Tapestry album measures 5x11 inches; moiré album measures 8x9½ inches.

MATERIALS
For tapestry album
Twelve 4½x10⅜-inch envelopes
Two 4¼x10⅝-inch mat boards
Two 5¾x11¾-inch pieces of tapestry fabric
Two 5¼x11⅝-inch pieces of coordinating wrapping paper for inside covers
⅛-inch-wide natural raffia
Three 12-inch-long tree twigs
Large-eyed needle

For moiré album
Twelve 7x8-inch sealable plastic bags
½ yard of pink moiré
½ yard of 1-inch-wide pink grosgrain ribbon
One 7¾x8¼-inch poster board
Two 8x8½-inch pieces and two 1x8-inch strips of mat board
2x8-inch strip of quilt batting
White paper; double-stick tape
Fabric fraying retardant
2 yards of pink perle cotton; tapestry needle

For both albums
Rubber cement; fabric glue
Nail and hammer
Paper clips or clothespins

INSTRUCTIONS
For the tapestry album
Fold a crease ½ inch from the bottom of each envelope, folding toward the envelope flap. With rubber cement, glue together the folded bottoms of three envelopes. Repeat, making four groups of three envelopes each. Use clothespins or paper clips to hold envelopes together until cement dries.

Referring to Figure 1, *below,* mark holes as indicated at the bottom of one set of envelopes. Working atop a wood block or stack of magazines, hammer a nail through each mark to punch holes in the envelopes. Use holes in first set to punch holes in remaining sets. Glue all envelopes together, aligning the punched holes.

INSIDE COVERS: Apply rubber cement to wrong side of wrapping paper; center one mat board atop each piece of wrapping paper. Apply rubber cement to the edges of the mat boards, then fold paper over boards; miter the corners. Let glue dry.

FRONT COVERS: Pull a thread on each side of the tapestry pieces to square the grain of the fabric; trim unsquared portion.

Position mat boards on the wrong side of the tapestry pieces with a ½-inch margin of fabric extending at the top, bottom, and one side of each board. Use fabric glue to adhere uncovered side of mat boards to the wrong side of the fabric. Place the two covers under heavy books while the glue dries overnight.

When glue is completely dry, pull threads in the ½-inch fabric margins to make fringe. The remaining side will be the binding edge.

ASSEMBLY: Lay one cover facedown on a flat surface. Place the envelopes atop the cover, centering them between the top and bottom edges of the board. Align the unglued long edge of the envelopes with the remaining side of the mat board where the fabric is fringed.
. Nail holes through the fabric to correspond with holes in envelopes.

Lay remaining cover atop envelopes, aligning it with the first cover. Clamp covers and envelopes together; make holes in second cover.

Thread needle with a 30-inch length of raffia; bring both ends together. Starting on the top side of the book, stitch raffia through one hole and back up through the second hole in the same pair. Leaving the raffia untied, slip needle off. Repeat for the remaining pairs of holes.

Lay tree twigs on book cover and tie each pair of raffia ends in a knot around the twigs to secure them. Trim ends to desired lengths. For added embellishment, we slipped a pair of brass washers onto the sticks before tying them down.

For the moiré album
CUTTING THE FABRIC: Cut two 9x42-inch strips of moiré. From one piece, cut an 8½x16-inch rectangle and two 9x9½-inch pieces. From the remaining fabric, cut one 8¾x9¼-inch piece, two 2x9-inch pieces for hinges, and one 6½x15-inch piece for the bow.

BACK COVER: Center an 8x8½-inch mat board on the wrong side of a 9x9½-inch piece of moiré; center a 1x8-inch mat board strip atop a hinge fabric piece. Fold fabric edges over boards and secure with fabric glue; fold corners to miter.

Place these two pieces side by side, fabric side down, with a ⅛-inch-wide gap between them.

Apply fabric fraying retardant to both ends of an 8½-inch length of ribbon. Center and glue ribbon over the gap to hold the two covered boards together.

Cover poster board in the same manner, centering it on an 8¾x9¼-inch piece of moiré. Let glue dry, then glue the poster board, right side up, to the uncovered side of the back cover. Set back cover aside to dry.

FRONT COVER: Cover the remaining mat board with moiré in the same manner as for the back cover. This will be the inside of the front cover.

Fold the batting in half lengthwise and glue it to one side of the remaining hinge board. Proceed to cover this hinge board with moiré as you did for the back hinge.

Machine-stitch ¼ inch from each long edge of the 8½x16-inch moiré. Pull horizontal threads out of the fabric edges to make fringe up to the stay stitching. Stitch or glue a ¼-inch hem on the remaining sides.

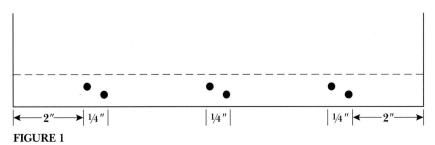

FIGURE 1

Glue the hemmed edges of this strip to the uncovered side of the front mat board; let glue dry. Pleat the excess fabric to fit the cover; press pleats flat. Glue pleats and outside edges in place. Attach hinge to front cover with ribbon in the same manner as for the back cover.

ASSEMBLY: Slip a 1x7-inch paper strip into the bottom of each plastic bag. With double-stick tape, tape bags together at bottom edges to keep them from slipping as you work. Use paper clips at the sides.

Working on a wooden block or stack of magazines, use a hammer and nail to punch four holes through the bottom of the bags, placing them ½ inch from the bottom and side edges and evenly spaced across the width. Drive corresponding holes through the hinge of the back cover.

Thread the perle cotton into the needle; knot the ends together. Put the needle into the first hole through the bags only. Slide the needle between the thread strands to create a loop; pull loop taut around the bags, burying the knot in the hole.

Put the needle through the first hole in the back hinge and around the outside edge of the hinge back to the top of the bags. Push the needle through the same hole, this time going through both bags and hinge.

Working from the back of the hinge, push needle through second hole of hinge and bags. Pull thread over the edge to the back and reinsert needle through same hole. Insert needle through third hole and repeat the process, wrapping the thread around the edges as before. When the fourth hole has been stitched, repeat the procedure in the opposite

direction through all holes. Tie off the perle cotton in a small knot at the first hole.

Glue the hinged section of the front cover over sewn edges of the bags, aligning edges of both covers.

BOW: Fold the 6½x15-inch strip of moiré in half, making a 3¼x15-inch rectangle with right sides together. Machine-stitch diagonally across the short ends; trim excess fabric, leaving a ¼-inch seam allowance.

Stitch the long edges together, leaving a small opening in the center for turning. Clip corners; turn right side out. Press strip, then hand-sew opening closed. Make an overhand knot to make a bow; glue knot to front cover.

Skinny Santa Cross-Stitched Hanging

Door hanger is 3x12¼ inches. Design stitch count is 22 wide and 133 high.

MATERIALS

5x14½ inches *each* of 14-count Aida cloth and fusible interfacing
4x13½-inch strip of red print fabric
Embroidery floss in colors listed in the color key, *opposite*
½ yard *each* of ¹⁄₁₆-inch-wide and ¼-inch-wide red satin ribbon
Three 8-mm gold-tone jingle bells
Pencil and ruler

INSTRUCTIONS

Using three strands of floss, center and stitch the Santa design on the Aida. The top of the design should be 1½ inches from the 5-inch edge.

When stitchery is complete, fuse interfacing to back of Aida. Trim the fabric to ¾ inch around the design at the top and sides; leave 2¼ inches of fabric at the bottom.

On the back of the fused piece, mark the center point of the bottom edge. On each side edge, make a mark 1½ inches from the bottom. Draw a diagonal line from each side mark to the bottom center mark. Cut the fused Aida on these lines.

Use the stitched piece as a pattern to cut the red fabric, cutting it ½ inch larger on all sides than the Aida. Center the stitchery on the red fabric with wrong sides together; baste.

Turn the edges of the red fabric over ¼ inch so they just touch the edge of the stitchery; clip corners as necessary to miter. Press. Turn the red fabric over another ¼ inch, encasing all raw edges. Topstitch.

Cut 6 inches of ¼-inch-wide ribbon. Tack ends of ribbon at the top corners on the back of the hanging.

From the ¹⁄₁₆-inch-wide ribbon, cut two 2-inch lengths and one 2½-inch piece. Thread each piece through the top opening of a bell. Fold ribbons in half and tack ends approximately 1¾ inches from the bottom point of the door hanger.

Tie the remaining wide ribbon into a 2-inch-wide bow; tack bow in place atop the ends of the bell hangers. Trim bow ends as desired.

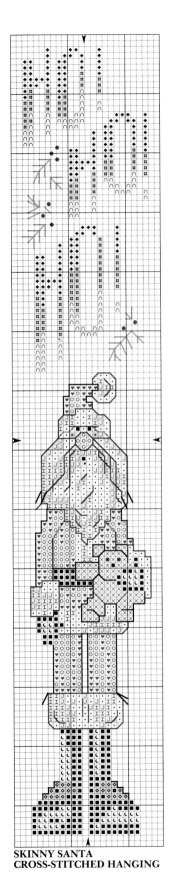

**SKINNY SANTA
CROSS-STITCHED HANGING**

Embellish a sweater with duplicate stitch

Another idea for this design is shown *above*. The "HO, HO, HO" motif is worked in duplicate stitch with six strands of red or green floss to turn a purchased stockinette-stitch sweater into a fun holiday garment (see page 66 for the duplicate stitch diagram). We worked straight stitches for the accompanying holly leaves and French knots for the red berries.

COLOR KEY

Anchor		DMC	
002	· ·	000	white
403	■ ■	310	black
047	O O	321	christmas red
401	C C	413	steel gray - dk
363	✕ ✕	436	tan
923	◆ ◆	699	christmas green - vy dk (alternate DMC color—815)
227	⌗ ⌗	701	christmas green - med dk (alternate DMC color—321)
238	∩ ∩	703	chartreuse (alternate DMC color—350)
128	J J	775	baby blue - lt
043	♥ ♥	815	garnet - med dk
075	✳ ✳	3733	dusty rose - med lt
976	I I	3752	antique blue - lt

Blended needle:

	◇ ◇		002 HL gold KREINIK BALGER® blending filament (4 strands) & 729 (1 strand)

Backstitch:

382		3371 shoe buckles, most of Santa's suit, hat & teddy bear (1 strand)
922		930 Santa's nose, most of Santa's beard, pom-pom & fur trim (1 strand)

922		930 bottom edge of Santa's hat (2 strands)
923		699 branches (2 strands)

Straight stitch:

922	╱	930 rest of Santa's beard & fur trim on pants (1 strand)
382	╱	3371 rest of Santa's suit & teddy bear (1 strand)

French knot:

047	●	321 berries (3 strands)
403	●	310 teddy bear's eyes (2 strands)

Fabrics and finished design sizes:

11 Aida, 12-1/8"h x 2"w
14 Aida, 9-1/2"h x 1-5/8"w
18 Aida, 7-3/8"h x 1-1/4"w
22 Hardanger, 6-1/8"h x 1"w

Country Folk Dolls

Dolls are approximately 13½ inches tall.

MATERIALS

⅛ yard of tea-dyed muslin for
    goose and dolls' heads, hands,
    and legs
¼ yard *each* of black solid and blue
    checked fabrics for clothing
10-inch square of tea-dyed utility
    muslin or osnaburg for the
    woman's apron
3x6-inch piece of black wool fabric
    for the man's hat
½ yard of narrow black cord or
    ribbon for the man's suspenders
¼ yard of ¼-inch-wide lace for the
    woman's collar
Brown acrylic paint and small brush
Polyester filling; hot-glue gun
One skein of embroidery floss for
    the woman's hair; scraps of string
Scraps of brown sheep's wool for
    the man's hair
6 inches of necklace chain for the
    man's watch chain
Tracing paper or template material
Two ¾-inch-diameter plastic rings
    for hanging (optional)

INSTRUCTIONS

Before cutting the blue checked fabric and lace for the dolls' clothing, see page 157 for tips on tea-dyeing. Dry and press fabrics before cutting.

Making the doll bodies

Trace head, leg, hand, and arm patterns, *opposite*, and the body pattern on page 138 onto tracing paper or translucent plastic template material. Make separate tracings for the man's and woman's bodies and legs. Cut out a paper or plastic template for each piece. These patterns include a ¼-inch-wide seam allowance.

Trace around each template on the *wrong* side of the appropriate fabric. For *each* doll, cut the number of each piece indicated on the pattern. Cut the arm and body pieces for both dolls from the checked fabric. Cut the head and hand pieces from muslin, as well as the woman's legs. Cut the man's legs from the black fabric.

BODY: For each doll, sew front and back body pieces together, leaving the bottom edges open. Join two

head pieces for each doll, leaving the bottom edges open. Clip seam allowances; turn all pieces right side out.

Stuff the bodies firmly. Hand-sew the bottom of the woman's body closed, turning the seam allowances to the inside of the body. Loosely baste the bottom edges of the man's body together to keep filling in place.

Turn under the raw edge at the bottom of each head and stuff firmly. Center the open end of a head atop the neck of each body and hand-sew the heads in place.

LEGS: For each doll, join leg pieces in pairs, leaving top edges open. Clip seam allowances; turn each leg right side out. Paint the bottom 1½ inches of the woman's legs with brown paint; let dry. Stuff the man's and woman's legs firmly to within ½ inch of the top of each leg.

Turn under the ¼-inch seam allowance at the top of the woman's legs. Hand-stitch the legs in place at the bottom of the woman's body.

Remove basting stitches from the bottom of the man's body; insert legs into the opening. Turn under the seam allowance at the bottom of the body; top-stitch through all layers.

ARMS: Sew two arm pieces together, joining the longest edges. Stitch three more arms in the same manner. Press the seam allowances open, then press under a ¼-inch hem at the bottom (straight) edge of each arm.

Overlap the hemmed bottom edge of each arm on the top (straight) edge of one hand piece; top-stitch each arm/hand unit together.

With right sides together, sew the inside seam of each arm. Start at the bottom of the hand, pivot at the thumb, and sew up to the underarm. Clip seam allowances; turn the arms right side out. Stuff the arms. (*Note:* The woman's hands are stuffed as they are; the man's hands are stuffed lightly and then top-stitched to make finger indentations. See photo *above.*)

continued

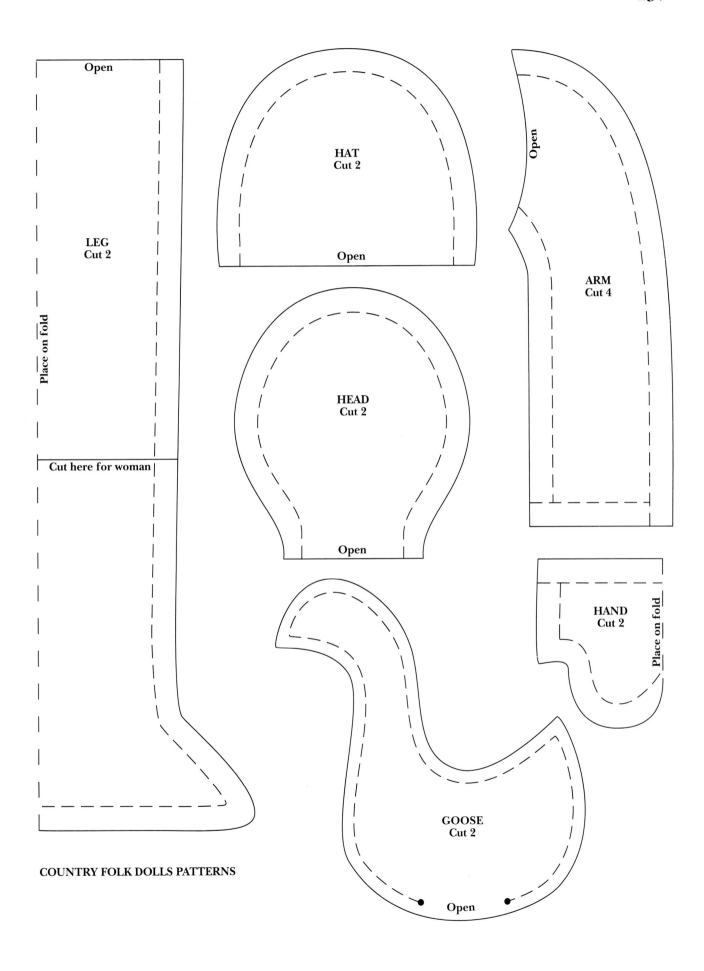

COUNTRY FOLK DOLLS PATTERNS

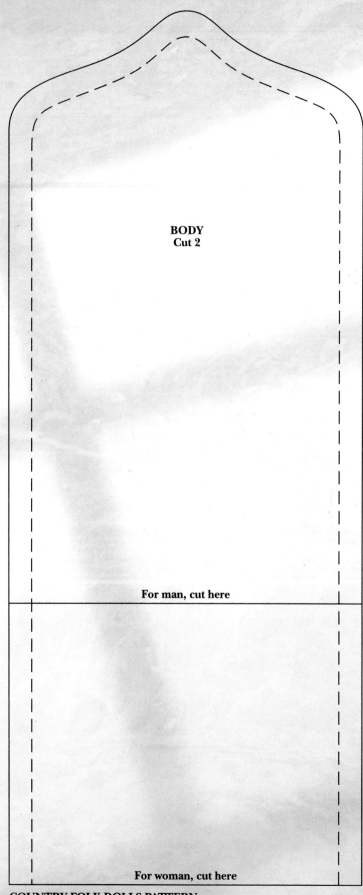

BODY
Cut 2

For man, cut here

For woman, cut here

COUNTRY FOLK DOLLS PATTERN

Turn under the seam allowance at the top of each sleeve. Hand-sew a sleeve in place at each shoulder.

Making the dolls' clothing

MAN'S PANTS: Cut two 4¼x8½-inch pieces of black fabric for the man's pants. Find the center of one short side in each piece. From this point, draw a 6¼-inch line parallel to the 8½-inch sides of the rectangle. Cut each pants piece on this line.

With right sides together, stitch the two pants pieces together at both sides. Then sew the inner leg seam around the slit, stitching from the bottom of one leg, up and around the top of the slit, and down to the bottom of the other leg. Trim and clip the seam allowances as necessary, then turn the pants right side out.

Turn under a ¼-inch hem at the waist and bottom of each pant leg; top-stitch leg hems. Pull pants onto doll; gather waist of pants to fit.

Cut the cording into two equal lengths. Tack one end of each piece to the front of the pants, spaced about 1 inch apart. Bring the cording over the shoulders, crisscrossing in the center back; tack the cording ends to the back waist of the pants.

Tack watch chain in place as shown in the photo on page 136.

HAT: Join the two hat pieces, leaving the bottom edges open. Trim and clip seam allowances; turn hat right side out. Turn up a ½-inch hem around the bottom edge; top-stitch.

Turn up the bottom edge ¼ inch to form a brim; tack brim in place.

Push a small amount of stuffing into the top of the hat. With hot-glue gun, glue hat on head. Glue sheep's wool to back and sides of head.

APRON: Cut a 4½-inch square for the apron skirt and a 2½x2¾-inch rectangle for the bib. Gather one edge of the skirt to fit one long edge of the bib; stitch skirt to bib.

Top-stitch a ¼-inch hem on all raw edges of the apron. Tack apron to body at top corners of bib, at the waist, and at both sides.

FINISHING: Leaving the manufacturer's bands in place on each end of the skein of floss, gather the strands together in the middle of the skein; tack the gathered center of the floss to the center top of the woman's head. Gather the floss strands at each side of the head (at ear level) and tack them to the fabric.

Remove the manufacturer's bands and cut the loops at each end. Braid the loose floss on each side. Secure the braids with string bows.

Tack or glue a collar of narrow lace around the woman's neck. Tie a tiny piece of fabric or ribbon in place for the man's bow tie.

Paint facial features on each doll as desired. If you wish to hang the dolls for display, hand-sew a small ring to the center back of each doll.

Making the goose

Trace the goose pattern on page 137, and make a paper pattern. Cut two goose pieces.

With right sides facing, sew the two pieces together, leaving an opening at the bottom as indicated on the pattern. Trim and clip seam allowances; turn goose right side out and stuff firmly. Close opening by hand.

Paint a brown beak and make a tiny dot on each side of the head for eyes.

Position goose under the woman's right arm; tack woman's right hand to body to keep goose snugly in place.

Gilded Eggs and Nest

MATERIALS

Assorted small wooden eggs
Sheets of gold leaf
24- to 36-point rub-on letters in desired type styles (available at art-supply stores)
Red base paint
Small paintbrush
Decorator's Gilt in red and patina
Jar of adhesive sizing
Satin-finish spray sealer
Gloss polyurethane spray or liquid (available at hardware stores)
Purchased shallow basket or nest
Assorted pinecones and feathers
Hot-glue gun; sandpaper

INSTRUCTIONS

Sand eggs smooth, then apply one coat of red base paint. When paint is dry, apply adhesive sizing, following manufacturer's instructions. Let the adhesive dry.

Apply gold leaf in small pieces. Rub off excess with dry brush. With your fingernail, scratch lines in the gold leaf to expose the red base coat. Rub eggs with red and patina gilt to achieve subtle highlights in coloring. Spray eggs with satin sealer; let dry.

Follow directions on package to apply rub-on letters, spelling out greetings or lines from your favorite carols. Spray eggs again with sealer; let dry.

Following the manufacturer's directions, apply an even coating of gloss polyurethane to each egg.

Glue feathers around basket rim as desired; add a cluster of pinecones to embellish the nest.

Wood Molding Accessories

MATERIALS

Decorative moldings (available at
    most hardware stores)
Crafts jewels, beads, and other trim,
    as desired
Acrylic paints or gold-leaf adhesive
Paintbrush; varnish
White crafts glue
Bonding cement
Pin or barrette backings
Adjustable suspender clips and
    belting fabric for belt

INSTRUCTIONS

The shape and design of your carved
molding may suggest paint colors
and trim. We painted an oval medallion to look like a sunflower and
glued little black beads in its center.
A coat of varnish sealed everything in
place. Silk leaves and a barrette clip
were glued to the back.

A feather-shape molding became a
fancy pin with a coat of gold-leaf adhesive, following directions on the
jar, and glued-on crafts jewels. We
used bonding cement to adhere a pin
clasp to the back of the wood piece.

BELT: To make a customized belt
with a medallion buckle, purchase
belting to fit around your waist plus
12 inches. Use only the two slides
from the packaged suspender clips.

Slip one end of belting through
one slide. Fold back 1 inch of fabric
and stitch through all layers to secure
the fabric to the slide. Hem opposite
end of belting as desired.

Glue slides to back of the painted
wood piece, allowing half the slide to
extend beyond the medallion edge.

To wear the belt, wrap the fabric
around your waist and pull the loose
end through the slide loop.

Collectible Santas
ALL THROUGH THE HOUSE

*Twas the night before
Christmas, and
strong was the need
To make something of clay,
of wood, or of tweed.
For the children were
tense, anxious with fear
That Old Nick's jolly face
might be absent this year.
But back in the work room
were Santas galore,
Teeming with charm, fun,
and humor and more.
Crafted with pride, from
these six great new ideas
For collectible Santas that
you'll cherish for years.
Add your own special touch
to a hand-crafted gnome,
And you'll find elfin magic
in your Christmas home.*

St. Nicholas Doll

Doll is approximately 14 inches tall.

MATERIALS
¼ yard of print fabric for doll's
    coat and hood (use a separate
    fabric for the hood if desired)
Two 5x9½-inch pieces of brown
    print fabric for the sack
Scraps of white, beige, tan, and
    flesh-colored fabrics for the
    beard, coat trim, glove, and face
Sewing threads in colors to match
    the fabrics
¼ yard *each* of muslin and batting
4-inch-diameter cardboard circle for
    base; fabric glue
Polyester fiberfill; spray starch
1-inch star-shaped appliqué or
    button; red pencil for cheeks
Tiny toys or packages for sack
¼ yard of paper-backed fusible
    webbing for machine appliqué
Nonpermanent fabric marker
Tracing paper and pencil

INSTRUCTIONS
Note: Patterns for the St. Nicholas
Doll are for machine appliqué as
shown. These patterns include seam
allowances only where a piece under-
lays another and on the doll's outside
edges where the front and back are
seamed. For hand appliqué, add a
¼-inch seam allowance when cutting
appliqué pieces.

Preparing body and sack fabrics
Trace the body pattern, *opposite* and
on page 144, joining the two parts of
the pattern as indicated. Trace all appliqué placement lines.
    Use the paper pattern to cut two
body pieces of muslin, one of batting,
and two of print fabric. Set aside one
print piece and one muslin piece for
the back of the doll.
    Mark appliqué placement lines on
the remaining print body piece. If
you have a light-colored fabric, trace
the lines by placing the fabric directly
over the marked pattern. If you are
working with a dark fabric, lay the
fabric atop the paper pattern taped
onto a brightly-lit window or a light
box so the pattern is visible through
the fabric.

continued

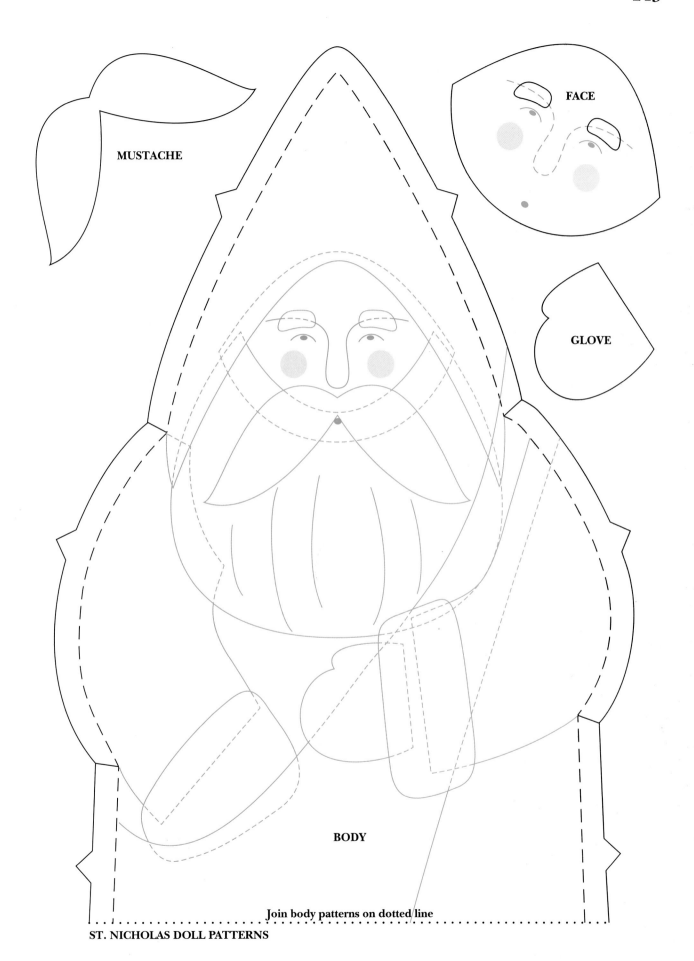

MUSTACHE

FACE

GLOVE

BODY

Join body patterns on dotted line

ST. NICHOLAS DOLL PATTERNS

Make a paper pattern for the sack piece in the same manner. With the wrong sides of the fabric together, lay the pattern atop the two pieces of brown fabric. Cut out the pattern shape through both layers of fabric.

Preparing the appliqué

Starch and press the remaining fabrics. Set aside a 5-inch square of beige fabric for the base before cutting the appliqué pieces.

MACHINE APPLIQUÉ: Trace the appliqué patterns on pages 143–145 onto the paper side of the fusible webbing; cut out each piece. For the trim at the bottom of the doll's coat, draw two 1x6¼-inch rectangles on the webbing.

Following the manufacturer's directions, fuse each piece of webbing to the *wrong* side of the appropriate appliqué fabric. Cut out each fused fabric piece, following the pattern lines drawn on the webbing.

HAND APPLIQUÉ: Make a paper pattern for each appliqué piece. Mark the outline of each pattern on the *right* side of the appropriate fabric. Cut out each appliqué piece, adding a ¼-inch seam allowance.

Turn under and press the seam allowances on each piece; to allow for proper overlapping, however, do not turn under an edge that will be covered by another piece, such as the edges of the face piece or the straight edge of the glove.

Appliquéing the doll

PLACEMENT: Using the placement lines drawn on the front body piece, position all pieces except the sack, glove, right sleeve, and right cuff. For hand appliqué, position pieces with pins or basting. For machine appliqué, fuse each piece in place.

Start with the face piece, then add the eyebrows, beard, and mustache. Position the left sleeve piece, slipping the top edge under the beard. Add the hood and left cuff.

STITCHING: Sandwich the batting between the prepared front piece and one muslin body piece; baste the three layers together.

continued

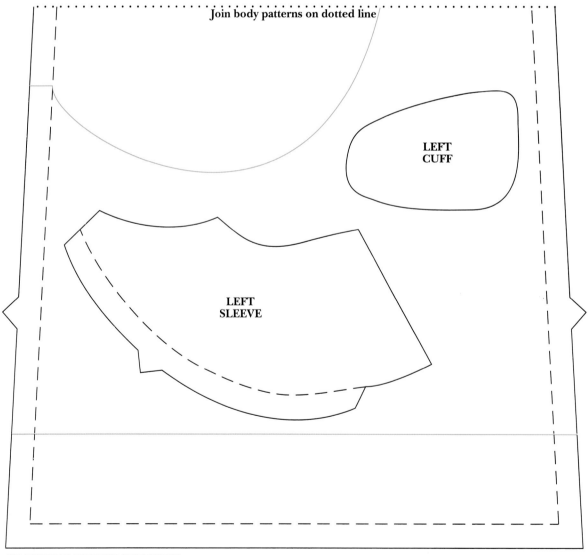

Join body patterns on dotted line

LEFT CUFF

LEFT SLEEVE

ST. NICHOLAS DOLL PATTERNS

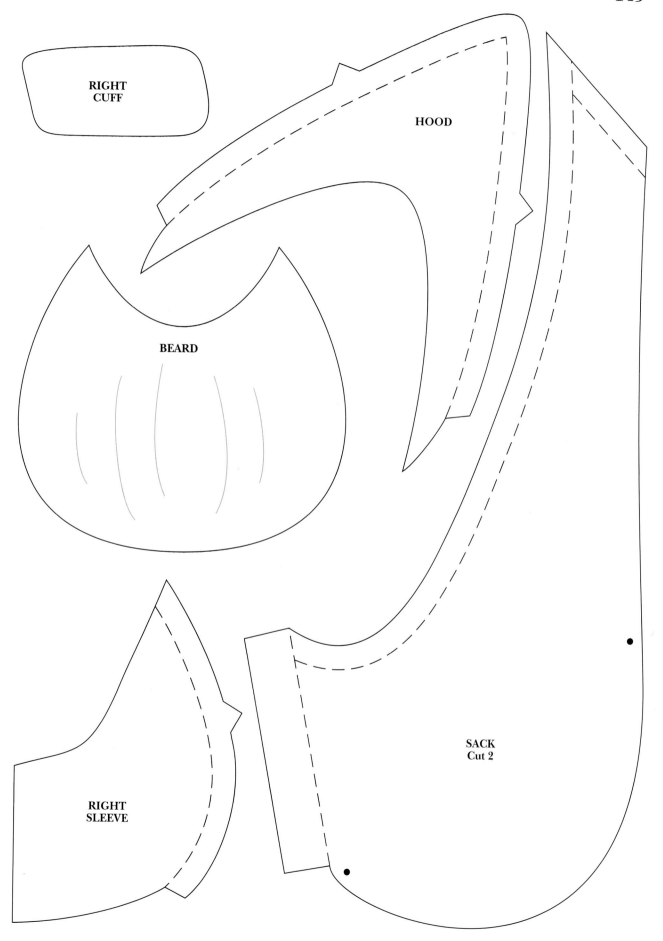

RIGHT
CUFF

HOOD

BEARD

RIGHT
SLEEVE

SACK
Cut 2

Work detail lines for the nose with a narrow machine-zigzag stitch, then hand-embroider satin stitches and straight stitches for the eyes before appliquéing the eyebrows.

Using threads that match each fabric, stitch the positioned pieces in place. For machine appliqué, use a tight, narrow zigzag (satin) stitch. To appliqué by hand, secure the edges with tiny blind stitches.

SACK: With right sides facing, sew the sack pieces together along the curved top seam line. Clip the seam allowances; turn right side out and press. Baste the unsewn bottom edges of the two pieces together.

Sewing by hand, slightly gather the bottom of the sack between the dots shown on the sack pattern. Pin the sack on the body front, leaving the top (seamed) edge of the sack very loose. Appliqué the bottom edge in place; remove basting thread.

FINISHING: Position the left sleeve, cuff, and glove on top of the sack; appliqué these pieces in place.

Line the back body piece with the remaining muslin body piece. Appliqué trim strips at the bottom of both the front and back bodies.

With right sides facing, baste the back body piece to the front body. Machine-stitch the bodies together, sewing from top to bottom on each side of the doll. Leave the bottom edge open. Reinforce stitching at corners and pivot points.

Clip seam allowances at curves; turn right side out. Stuff body firmly.

Trim the cardboard base as necessary to fit snugly inside the bottom of the doll. From the fabric square set aside for the base, cut a circle ¼ inch larger than the cardboard circle.

Center and glue the cardboard to the wrong side of the fabric circle. Make small clips in the fabric up to the cardboard. Glue the clipped fabric over the edge of the cardboard.

Turn up the seam allowance at the bottom of the body. Slip the base into the opening; whipstitch base in place.

Stuff the bottom of the sack with a little polyester fiberfill. Glue small toys or packages in the sack and the star to the top of the hood. Use red pencil to lightly tint the doll's cheeks.

Big-Pocket Santa Doll

Doll is approximately 20 inches tall.

MATERIALS
20-inch square of napped fabric for doll's legs and body (we used a wine-colored, thin-waled corduroy; velveteen or velour are good substitutes)

¾ yard of heavy, coarse cotton fabric for the coat

¼ yard of imitation fur for boots

⅓ yard of green stretch-velour for arms and hat

8-inch square of ivory knit fabric for the head

1¼ yards of ⅜-inch-diameter sisal rope for beard

1⅔ yards of ½-inch-wide woven cotton trim for coat hem and belt

2 yards of cording for boot trim

One skein of perle cotton or lightweight yarn for boot laces

Two small bells for boots

Three small pom-poms for hat tip

Two small black beads for eyes

Ivory, red, and black sewing thread

Polyester fiberfill; carpet thread

Powdered blush or red pencil for cheeks

Stiff hairbrush; white crafts glue

Compass or 7-inch-diameter circle template; graph paper and ruler

Tracing paper and pencil

Imitation greens for pockets and hat trim; tiny toys for pockets

INSTRUCTIONS
Preparing the patterns
Trace patterns for the hat, boot, arm, and pocket on pages 148 and 149. Include all markings, including nap direction lines.

For the coat, use a ruler to draw a 6⅞x14-inch rectangle on graph paper. Trace the armhole curve from the coat pattern on page 149; tape the tracing atop the upper right corner of the rectangle to complete the pattern. Mark fold indications at top and left sides as shown on the pattern. Mark the pocket placement as shown; the lowest point of the pocket outline should be 1¼ inches from the bottom of the coat pattern.

Refer to the illustration *below* to draw a pattern for the legs on graph paper. Cut out all seven paper patterns. These patterns include ¼-inch seam allowances.

Cutting the fabrics
Cut two legs from the corduroy, placing the pattern parallel to the nap of the fabric. For the chest/tummy, cut a 6x8-inch rectangle from the remaining corduroy with the nap parallel to the 6-inch sides.

From the fur, cut two of the boot top pattern, two of the boot side pattern with the markings faceup, and two more side pieces with the markings facedown. Position the patterns with the nap direction as indicated.

From the remaining fur, cut two 2x9-inch strips for the ankle wraps, with the nap of the fur parallel to the 2-inch sides.

For the coat, cut one 16x32-inch rectangle. Fold this piece in half so that it measures 16 inches square; fold again to obtain a quartered piece that measures 8x16 inches. Position the fabric so the 8-inch folded edge is at the top and the 16-inch folded edge is along the left side. Lay the pattern atop the fabric, aligning it with the folds at the top and left side. Cut the fabric at the bottom and right edges of the pattern.

Cut two 9x10-inch rectangles of coat fabric for sleeves, two 2x4½-inch strips for cuffs, and two pockets.

From the green velour, cut one of the hat pattern; set aside the remaining velour for the arms.

continued on page 150

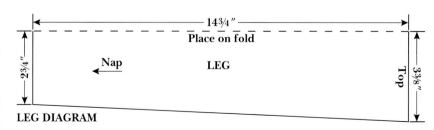

LEG DIAGRAM

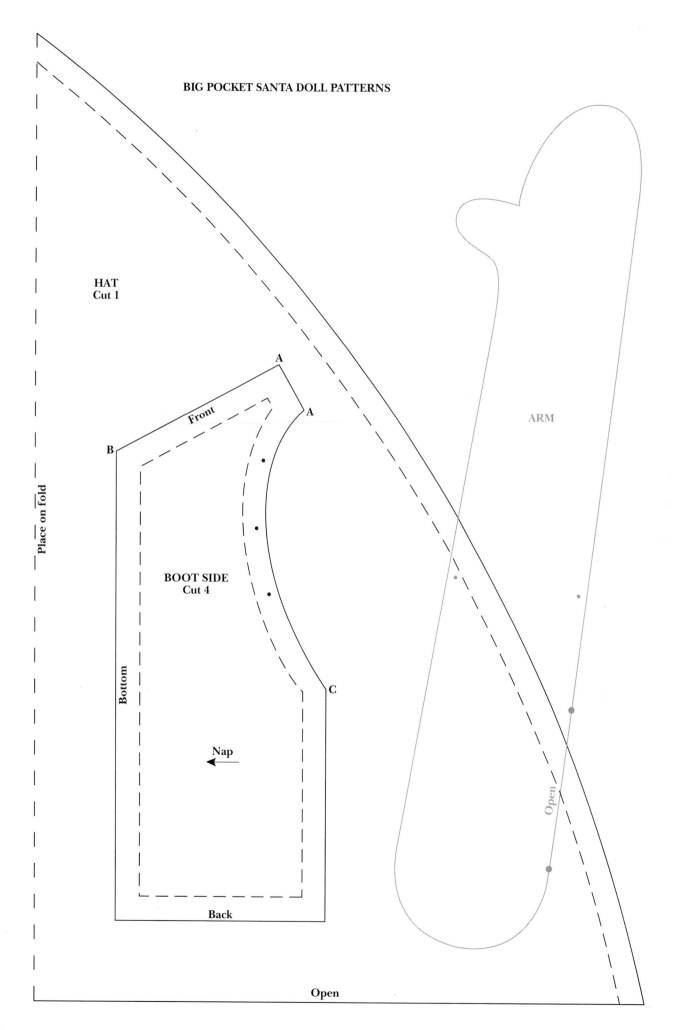

BIG POCKET SANTA DOLL PATTERNS

HAT
Cut 1

Place on fold

A

Front

A

B

BOOT SIDE
Cut 4

Bottom

C

Nap

Back

ARM

Open

Open

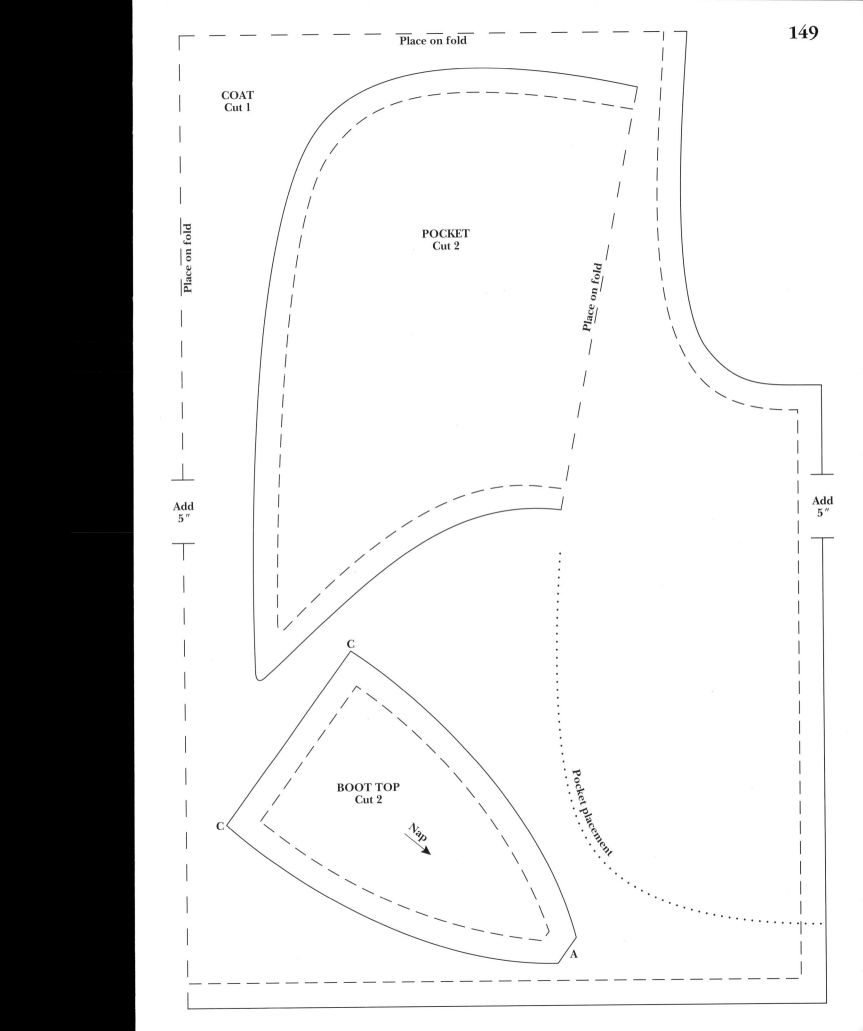

COAT
Cut 1

Place on fold

Place on fold

Place on fold

POCKET
Cut 2

Add
5″

Add
5″

C

C

BOOT TOP
Cut 2

Nap

Pocket placement

A

Assembling the legs and boots

LEGS: With right sides facing, stitch the long edges of one leg piece together, leaving an opening in the center of the seam for stuffing.

Flatten the leg, positioning the seam at the center back. Stitch the top edges together. Turn leg right side out. Prepare the second leg in the same manner.

Push stuffing into the lower part of each leg through the open end.

BOOTS: With right sides facing, join two side pieces by stitching along the edge marked "A–B" on the pattern. Set in a boot top piece, stitching from "A" to "C" on both sides.

Sew the back edges together, then stitch the bottom edges.

With the boot still wrong side out, match the back and front seams with the bottom seam. This should create a triangle at both ends of the boot as illustrated in Figure 1, *below.*

Referring to the illustration, stitch across the back seam ½ inch from the tip of the triangle, then sew across the front seam ⅜ inch from the tip. Cut off the bulky points of both triangles, leaving a ¼-inch seam allowance. Turn boot right side out.

Make the second boot in the same manner. Brush the fur over the boot seams. Firmly stuff both boots.

Slip a boot onto the bottom of each leg. Hand-sew the top of each boot to the leg.

EMBELLISHING THE BOOTS: To simulate lacing, use two strands of perle cotton to stitch across the top of each boot at the points indicated by dots on the pattern.

Sew or glue cording over the seam around the top of each boot. Sew bells to the toes.

Wrap a 2x9-inch fur strip around each ankle. Overlap the ends of each strip at the back of the leg; hand-sew the edges together. Cut the remaining cording in half. Wrap one piece around the fur at each ankle.

JOINING THE LEGS: Through the opening in each leg seam, continue to add stuffing until legs are very firm. Hand-sew the opening closed.

Place the legs side by side, toes pointed forward. Starting at the front top and working down 7 inches, hand-sew the legs together; repeat from the back.

Adding the chest/tummy piece

Fold the 6x8-inch piece of corduroy in half with right sides facing, making a piece 6x4 inches. Stitch the three sides, leaving an opening for turning. Turn the piece right side out and stuff. Hand-sew the opening closed.

Referring to the photo, *above,* position the stuffed rectangle atop the joined legs, centering one 4-inch side 1 inch below the top of the joined legs. Tack the corners of the rectangle to the legs.

Making the arms

On the wrong side of one velour piece, trace two outlines of the arm pattern, spacing them at least ½ inch apart. Machine-stitch through two layers of fabric on the drawn lines, leaving an opening in one side of each arm as indicated on the pattern.

Cut out two arms, leaving ¼-inch seam allowances. Clip curves; turn right side out. Stuff arms until they are moderately firm but still pliable; hand-sew the arm openings closed.

In the middle of each arm (indicated by dots on the pattern), pinch the two side seams together to make an elbow fold; tack folds in place.

Pin the arms to the sides of the legs at the top. Use carpet thread to whipstitch arms in place. The completed body is shown in the photo at *left.*

Making the coat

Cut a front opening in the coat piece along one vertical fold line, stopping 1 inch from the shoulder fold.

With right sides facing, stitch one 9-inch side of a sleeve rectangle into each armhole, easing the sleeve to fit.

Gather the bottom edge of each sleeve. With right sides facing, stitch a cuff strip to the gathered edge of each sleeve.

Sew the side/underarm seam on each side of the coat, sewing from the bottom edge of the coat to the end of the cuff strip. Turn under a ¼-inch hem at the bottom of the cuff, then turn the cuff in half to the inside of the coat; whipstitch the turned edge in place to secure the hem.

At the bottom edge of the coat, turn up a ¼-inch hem on the *outside* of the coat; topstitch. Hem both sides of the center opening in the same manner. Fold the edges of the center opening back again, folding over approximately 1 inch at the bottom of the coat and tapering the fold to only ⅛ inch near the top of the slit. Topstitch the folds in place.

Sew or glue a strip of woven trim around the bottom edge of the coat, covering the turned-up hem.

ADDING POCKETS: Press under the seam allowances around all edges of both pockets. Gather the bottom curve of each pocket.

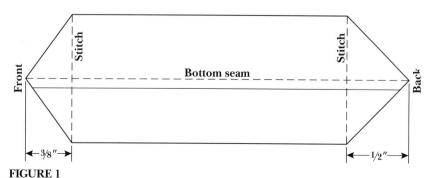

FIGURE 1

Pin a pocket on each coat front as indicated on the pattern. (Pockets extend to back of coat following the pocket placement markings.) Topstitch pockets to coat, leaving tops of pockets open.

FITTING COAT ON BODY: Run a gathering thread across the shoulder fold of the coat and another row of gathers at the waist, 8 inches from the bottom edge.

Drape coat over body, aligning the shoulder fold with the top edge of the chest/tummy piece. Gather the coat fabric at the shoulders so the armhole seams line up with the edge of the legs and tack in place. Pull gathers at waist tight and knot the gathering thread to secure it. Adjust all gathers as necessary to give the coat a bloused look. In three or four spots, tack waist gathers to body.

Tie the remaining length of woven trim around the waist for a belt. Tack the hands to the waist, hooking the doll's thumbs into the belt.

Fill pockets with tiny toys and imitation greens as desired.

Making the doll's head
Cut a 7-inch-diameter circle of ivory knit fabric for the head. Gather the edges and stuff the fabric with filling until you have a firm oval shape. Whip the open edges closed at the back of the head.

To make a nose, pinch a ½-inch-wide section forward at the center front of the head. Referring to Figure 2, *above, right,* use white or ivory thread to stitch through the fabric and into the filling. In the illustration, each dash represents one stitch. Stitch from one side of the nose to the other, pulling each stitch tight.

Use a single strand of black thread to make a straight stitch for each eyebrow and sew a bead in place for each eye. Use a doubled strand of red thread to work straight stitches for the mouth.

FIGURE 2

Make circles of color for cheeks, using blush or colored pencil.

Use carpet thread to sew the bottom one-third of the head atop the coat, stitching into the body as much as possible.

Making the hair and beard
Cut ten 8-inch lengths of sisal rope. Untwist each piece and soak it briefly in water. Wrap each piece around the shaft of a pencil. When completely dry, remove the pencil and gently spread the curls apart.

Arrange five strands of curls at the bottom of the head for a beard. Use one strand of sewing thread to tack the sisal to the head. For the hair, spread two more curls across the top of the head close to the eyebrows.

Pull a few strands from one of the remaining curls; stitch these under the nose for a mustache. Stitch the remaining sisal around the back of the head.

Making the hat
With right sides facing, stitch the curved edges of the hat together. Turn the hat right side out. Stitch pom-poms to hat tip.

Turn under a 1-inch hem at the bottom edge of the hat; sew or glue the hem in place.

Slip hat over doll's head and tack it in several places. Fold down the hat tip to one side; tack tip to side of head. Glue imitation holly in place.

Papier-mâché Santa

Shown on page 152.
Figure is approximately 12 inches tall.

MATERIALS
To make one figure
1-pound package of papier-mâché powdered mix (we used Celluclay Instant Papier-Mâché)
Mixing bowl or large plastic bag
Spoon-shaped leather tool
12-inch-tall plastic foam cone
90 to 110 inches of 19-gauge steel or copper wire; wire cutters
Acrylic paints in dark red, gold, dark green, ivory, and flesh color
Small paintbrush; stencil brush
Clear matte acrylic spray
Antiquing medium; crafts glue
Toothpicks; butter knife

INSTRUCTIONS
Different embellishments create an individual personality for each of these Santas, but they all are made the same way.

Mixing the papier-mâché
Pour one-fourth of the papier-mâché powder into a mixing bowl or large plastic bag (the bag holds in dust that rises from the mix). Following the manufacturer's directions, add water and knead the mixture to a claylike consistency. Note package directions for proper storage of powder and unused portions of prepared clay.

Applying the papier-mâché clay
Firmly press a marble-size ball of clay onto the cone. Dip your hands in warm water, then use your wet fingers to smooth the clay in a thin layer over the surface of the cone. Continue adding clay in this manner until the cone is completely covered.

Mark a spot for the face near the top of the cone by making a thumbprint in the damp clay.

To outline the edge of Santa's red coat, use a toothpick to draw an inverted V-shape in the clay, positioning the point of the V just under the face and drawing down to the bottom edge of the cone. Use the straight edge of a butter knife to make a slight indentation along this line, pressing into the foam.

continued

Shaping the hood and face

Use the back of the leather tool to make small indentations at the top of the face area for the eyes (these will be painted later).

Roll three tiny clay balls for facial features, making one for the nose smaller than the two for the cheeks. Blend these in under the eyes.

For the hood, flatten a ball of clay into a 2-inch-diameter circle ⅛ inch thick. Blend this into the clay at the top of the cone, using wet fingers and the leather tool to smooth the edges at the back and sides. Shape the front edges of the hood around the face.

Blend a small triangle of clay at the back of the cone and shape it to a point for the top of the hood.

Shaping the beard and arms

Roll clay between your hands to make a long tube. Blend this into the clay under the cheeks for the beard. Make a small opening just under the nose to paint in an O-shaped mouth.

Shape the beard, snakelike, down the front of the Santa. Use the leather tool to add texture to the beard; when antiquing medium is added, this texturing will be more visual.

Roll out two tubes of clay about 2 inches in diameter and 3½ inches long for the arms. Attach a tube to each side of the cone at shoulder height, positioning arms as desired. Use the leather tool to blend the clay securely into the clay on the cone.

With your finger, form a hole in the unattached end of each arm, making openings for the mittens. Spread the clay at the end of each arm into a bell shape.

Push a 1-inch length of wire into each hole, lodging half of it in the arm (and into the foam cone if the arm position allows). Shape two clay mittens; push one onto each exposed wire. Use the tip of the leather tool to blend the clay of the mittens into the clay of the arms, using the tip of the leather tool.

Painting and finishing

Shape clay into embellishments and accessories as desired. For our three Santas, we made hearts, balls, canes, a miniature tree, a round wreath, and a sack. These can be attached to the body or hands of the Santa, or added with wire later.

Let the clay dry for about two days, then apply a coat of glue (thinned with water) to all surfaces. Let glue dry for two hours before painting.

Referring to the photo, *above,* paint Santa and accessories as desired; mix red and ivory paints to make pink for the face. When paint is dry, spray with acrylic sealer; let dry. Follow the manufacturer's instructions to apply antiquing medium; when dry, apply another coat of acrylic sealer.

Cut 30 to 40 inches of wire for each figure. Wrap wire around the figure haphazardly as shown, attaching accessories as desired. To make tight curls in the wire, wrap the wire around a pencil.

Wooden Egg Santas

MATERIALS

For one set of three Santas

One *each* of 2½-, 4-, and 5½-inch tall wooden eggs (available from Unfinished Business, Box 246, Dept. BHG, Wingate, NC 28174)

3½ yards of tan No. 3 perle cotton

Two *each* of 10 mm and 14 mm gold-tone bells

Acrylic paints in flesh, dark red, black, and white

Two 1-inch foam brushes

One small paintbrush for details

One medium rounded paintbrush

Antiquing medium

Paint thinner; sandpaper

Matte acrylic spray

Paper towels

One jar of texture paste

Three small sprigs of fine artificial greenery

Assorted small twigs

Band saw

INSTRUCTIONS

Use a band saw to cut off the wider rounded end of each egg; cut just enough to create a flat surface so the egg will sit upright. Sand the rough edges smooth.

Painting the eggs

Use a foam brush to apply a circle of flesh-colored paint between the top and the middle of each egg. Let the paint dry for 5 minutes, then paint the rest of each egg dark red.

Use the rounded brush to swirl texture paste around each face, making beards, mustaches, and fur hood trims. Apply paste down the center fronts of the Santas for coat trim. When the paste is dry, go over it lightly with white paint. Let paint dry.

Use the detail brush to add black eyes and white eyebrows to each face. Lighten a small amount of dark red paint with a drop of white paint; use your fingertip to dab on a suggestion of cheek color. Let paint dry.

Mix antiquing medium with a little paint thinner to obtain a nice consistency for brush strokes. Using a foam brush, spread the antiquing mixture on all pieces. After approximately 5 minutes, wipe off excess medium with paper towels. Wait 1 hour, then spray the Santas with matte acrylic spray; let the spray dry for at least 5 minutes before handling the eggs.

Adding decorative details

Cut three 24-inch lengths of perle cotton. Tie them loosely around the largest Santa's "waist," knotting the strands together. Push a piece of greenery and a bundle of small twigs under the knot, adding a little glue to hold them in place. Let glue dry. Tie the 14 mm bells onto the ends of two strands of perle cotton.

Use two 18-inch-long pieces of perle cotton and the 10 mm bells to finish the medium-size Santa in the same manner. The smallest Santa has a one-strand belt with no bells.

Jolly Plaid Santa Doll

Doll is approximately 14½ inches tall.

MATERIALS
⅓ yard of 54-inch-wide plaid wool fabric
13-inch square of muslin
One 9x12-inch square *each* of green and yellow felt
2x13-inch strip of imitation fur for the hatband
⅔ yard of narrow woven ribbon for the hatband and sleeves
8 inches of ¼-inch sisal rope for the beard
Two ¼-inch-diameter black beads for eyes; one 15 mm jingle bell
Twigs for bag
Polyester fiberfill
Package of dried beans
18 inches of narrow twine for bag
Red acrylic paint; white crafts glue
Tea for staining muslin; sponge
Needle; black and ecru threads
Tracing paper, ruler, and pencil

INSTRUCTIONS
Preparing the patterns
Note: The patterns for the Santa's body, arms, nose, and face, *opposite* and on page 156, include ¼-inch seam allowances. The hat, star, and mitten patterns are actual size; seam allowances are added to these pieces *after* they are sewn.

Trace the patterns, then cut each shape from tracing paper. To cut a complete pattern for the body and star pieces, fold the tracing paper on the dotted lines and cut the paper on the solid lines through both layers.

Cutting the plaid fabric
Fold the plaid fabric in half, wrong sides together, so the piece measures 12x27 inches. Matching the fold line of the body pattern with the fold of the fabric, cut one body piece.

Cut two 8-inch squares for the hat. On one of these squares, draw the outline of the hat pattern, but do not cut it yet. Set the squares aside.

From the remaining plaid fabric, cut four of the arm pattern and one 7-inch-diameter circle for the base.

Making the Santa's body
With right sides together, stitch the center back seam of the body.

Pin the base to the bottom of body piece, matching right sides and raw edges; stitch. Clip the seam allowance as necessary, then turn the body right side out.

Pour a 1-inch layer of beans into the bottom of the body. Stuff the rest of the body with fiberfill until firm.

Making the Santa's hat
With wrong sides of the two 8-inch squares together and the outline of the hat faceup, stitch through both layers atop the drawn line. Leave bottom of the hat open as indicated on the pattern.

Trim the excess fabric, leaving a ¼-inch seam allowance. Cut carefully between the narrow spaces between seam lines. Clip curves to allow the seam allowance to spread, then turn the hat right side out. Hand-sew the bell to the hat tip.

Stuff the hat with fiberfill to within 2 inches of the bottom edge. Center the hat on the body with its seams at the sides and following the hat position line on the body pattern. Whip-stitch hat to body.

Making the Santa's face
Set aside one 8½x13-inch piece of muslin for the bag. From the remaining muslin, cut one of the face pattern, one nose, and two 2½-inch-diameter cheek circles.

Turn the edges of the face piece under ¼ inch and press. Pin face to center front of body, aligning the top of the face piece with the bottom of the hat. Blindstitch the face in place.

Hand-sew a gathering stitch all around the nose piece, ¼ inch from the edge. Stuff the nose lightly with fiberfill, pulling the gathering thread
continued

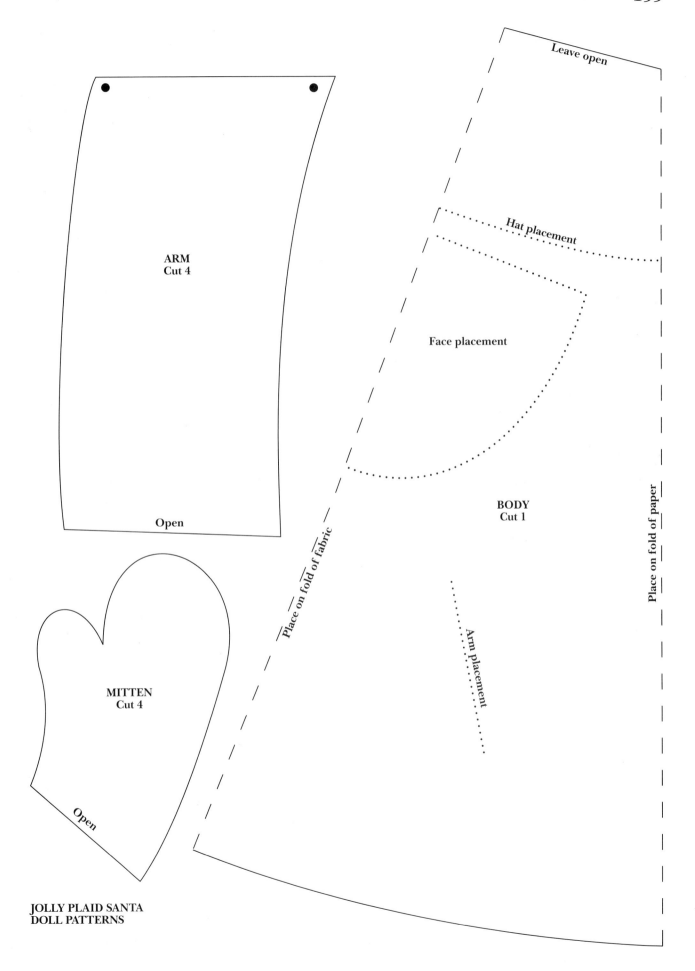

ARM
Cut 4

Open

Leave open

Hat placement

Face placement

BODY
Cut 1

Place on fold of fabric

Place on fold of paper

Arm placement

MITTEN
Cut 4

Open

**JOLLY PLAID SANTA
DOLL PATTERNS**

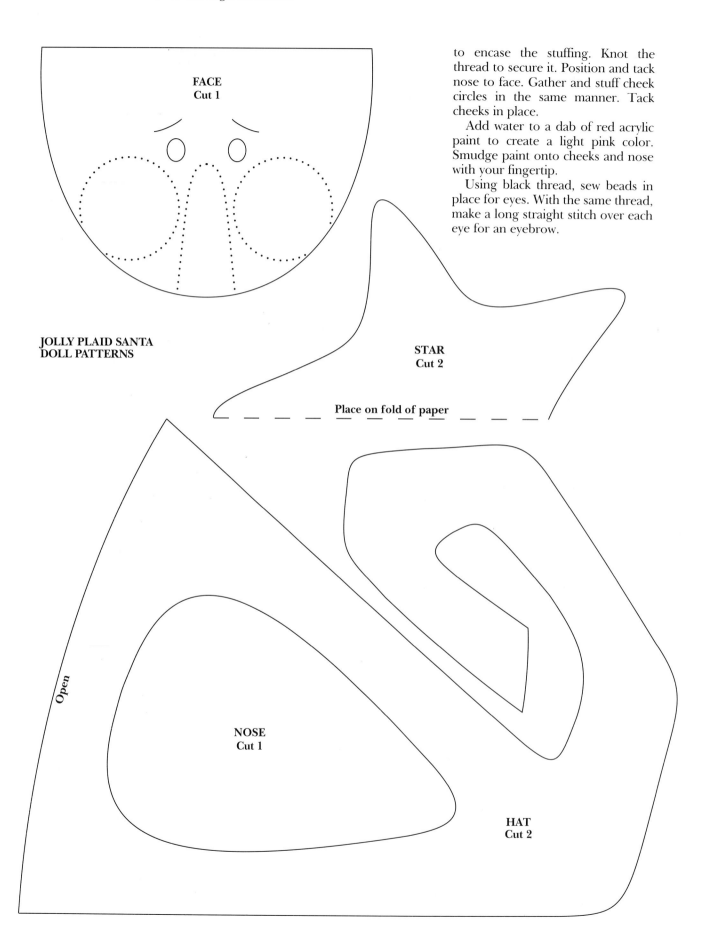

FACE
Cut 1

**JOLLY PLAID SANTA
DOLL PATTERNS**

STAR
Cut 2

Place on fold of paper

Open

NOSE
Cut 1

HAT
Cut 2

to encase the stuffing. Knot the thread to secure it. Position and tack nose to face. Gather and stuff cheek circles in the same manner. Tack cheeks in place.

Add water to a dab of red acrylic paint to create a light pink color. Smudge paint onto cheeks and nose with your fingertip.

Using black thread, sew beads in place for eyes. With the same thread, make a long straight stitch over each eye for an eyebrow.

Adding the beard
Separate the sisal into three strands. Untwist each strand and soak it separately in water. Wrap each wet strand around a pencil, tying it with thread to secure it around the pencil while it dries. Remove pencils when dry.

Gently spread each strand to open up the curls. Lay one section on the left side of Santa's head, beginning at the bottom of the hat. Spread the next section on the right side and the third section under the chin and nose to fill in the beard. Use ecru thread to randomly tack curls onto the face.

Glue the fur strip around the bottom of the hat to cover the top of the face and beard; let glue dry. Center 18 inches of woven ribbon around the fur; tie it in a bow at one side.

Making the arms and mittens
Sew the arm pieces together in pairs, leaving one end open for turning. Turn right side out; lightly stuff arms.

Lay the mitten pattern atop a double thickness of green felt; draw around the shape. Reposition the pattern and draw a second mitten. Sew on the drawn lines through both layers, leaving ends open. Trim fabric close to the stitching; stuff lightly.

Insert a mitten into the open end of each arm; fold under the edge of the arm opening and topstitch mittens and arms together. Cover each joint with a piece of woven ribbon.

Referring to the body pattern, position arms on body; tack corners of arms to body.

Trace the star pattern on yellow felt. Stitch on the drawn line through two layers of the felt; cut out the star close to the stitching. Carefully make a slit in one side of the star and insert fiberfill; be sure to push filling into each point. Sew slit closed.

Glue the finished star onto the palm of one mitten and to the top of the other mitten as pictured.

Making the Santa's bag
See the tips on tea-dyeing, *below*, to prepare the 8½x13-inch muslin for the bag. Dry the fabric before sewing.

Fold the muslin in half to measure 8½x6½ inches. Stitch across the bottom and side; turn bag right side out. We left the remaining edge raw, but you can ravel or pink it, if you prefer.

Fill the bag as desired with fiberfill and twigs; tie twine below the top edge of the bag to hold twigs in place. Tack bag to Santa's back.

Tips for Tea-Dyeing Fabric

Some crafters of folk-style dolls achieve the sepia tone of antique fabric by tea-dyeing—dipping fabric in tea to stain it. This works particularly well with muslin and other light-colored solid fabrics and laces, but also can be used for dark-colored or printed fabrics. Cotton fabric absorbs the tea stain better than polyester blends.

To begin, fill a 1-gallon container half full of very hot tap water. Add 16 tea bags; let tea bags steep for 20 minutes. Remove bags and stir. To use instant tea, mix it at twice the recommended strength.

Soak fabric and/or trims in the tea until the desired stain is achieved (usually about 30 minutes). The fabric will dry lighter than it appears while wet.

There are several techniques for creating a mottled look, which may seem more authentically antique. Some crafters wrap rubber bands tightly around randomly selected sections of the fabric to prevent even distribution of the stain. Others use a paintbrush to randomly apply tea to the fabric.

Another method for achieving a mottled look requires sealing the wet and crumpled tea-stained fabric in a plastic bag that is then placed in the freezer overnight. The cold causes the stain to migrate to certain areas and away from others. When thawed and pressed, the fabric looks old and randomly stained.

Knitted Santa Doll

Shown on page 158.
Doll measures 12½ inches tall.

MATERIALS
Brunswick Pomfret sport yarn (50-gram or 175-yard skein): one skein *each* of cardinal red (No. 524), ecru (No. 5000), pale pink (No. 5006), green (No. 544), and black (No. 560)
Straight knitting needles, sizes 4 and 5, or size to obtain gauge
Four double-pointed needles (dpn), sizes 4 and 5
Two stitch holders; one marker
Size E crochet hook
Yarn needle; tapestry needle
Blue and red embroidery floss
Polyester fiberfill
Sewing needle; white thread
Powdered blush or red crayon for cheek coloring

Abbreviations: See page 67.
Gauge: In st st with larger size needle, 6 sts and 8 rows = 1 inch.

INSTRUCTIONS
Note: To work the doll, knit every round (rnd) with dpns for st st. The doll's coat is worked back and forth in st st and color pattern following Chart 2 on page 159. While working the chart, read RS rows from right to left and WS rows from left to right. Carry color not in use loosely across WS of work. Twist the strands at the color changes to prevent holes.

Knitting the doll body
LEGS: Beginning at the boot with black and larger dpns, cast on 8 sts. Arrange sts onto 3 dpns; join, keeping sts untwisted, k 1 rnd.

Inc rnd: * K 1, yo; rep from * around.

Rnd 2: K around, working through back loop in each yo of previous rnd.

K 18 rnds even. Complete Chart 1 on page 159. With black k 3 rnd.

For upper leg, change to red; k 28 rnds.

Bind off 2 sts at the beg of next rnd and place rem sts on a holder. Make a second leg as described above but do not place these stitches on holder;

continued

rather, k around sts of first leg, matching bound-off sts of both to make the crotch. Rearrange the 28 sts onto dpns.

BODY: With red, k 7 sts; place marker (pm) to indicate beg of rnd. K 12 rnds. Change to ecru; k 12 rnds.

FRONT AND BACK: K 14 sts, cast on 1 st. Place rem 14 sts for Back onto a holder. Turn, p 15 sts, cast on 1 st. Work back and forth in st st on the 16 sts for 8 more rows. Bind off.

Work back as for Front.

ARMS (make two): With larger dpns and pink, cast on 7 sts. Arrange on 3 needles; join. K 1 rnd. Work inc rnds 1 and 2 as for leg—14 sts. K 9 rnds. Change to ecru and work 25 rnds. Bind off.

HEAD: With the larger dpns and pink, cast on 24 sts. Arrange on three needles; join. K 21 rnds.

Dec rnd 1: K 2, k 2 tog around.
Rnd 2: K 1, k 2 tog around.
Rnd 3: K 2 tog around.

Break off yarn, leaving an 18-inch end. Thread this strand through the tapestry needle and pull through rem 6 sts to gather. Fasten off.

FINISHING: Gather hands and feet closed, sew crotch seam, then stuff body with fiberfill.

Tack top of each foot to ankle. Sew shoulder seams (across five stitches), leaving an opening for head. Stuff arms and insert into armhole openings, securing in place.

Stuff head and run a gathering thread about ½ inch from bottom edge. Insert head into neck opening; stitch in place.

Adding Santa's hair and beard
HAIR: Cut sixty-eight 5-inch-long strands of ecru yarn for the hair and beard. Use sewing thread to stitch 12 strands, folded in half, to top of head on each side of a center part. Trim strands even at front and back.

BEARD: Sew the remaining strands, one at a time, onto the face with a stitch at the center of each strand; place the strands in a semicircle around the chin. Fill out the beard by adding more layers over the first semicircle, moving up the face.

Cut three 2-inch-long strands of ecru yarn for the mustache. Attach these to the face above the beard with a stitch in the center of each strand. Trim beard and mustache even.

FACE: Use ecru yarn to make two straight stitches, one above the other, for each eyebrow.

With blue embroidery floss, make French knots for eyes. With red floss, work two straight stitches for the mouth. Redden the cheeks with light circles of blush or red crayon.

Making Santa's coat
With smaller straight needles and green yarn, cast on 48 sts.

BORDER: K 2 rows green, k 2 rows ecru, k 2 rows green. Break off green. Change to larger needles and st st. With red and ecru yarn, follow Chart 2, *left.* Work even to 6 inches from beg, ending with a p row.

RIGHT FRONT: K across 11 sts, cast on 1 st. Place rem 37 sts on a holder to be worked later. Work established pat on 12 sts for 11 rows. Bind off 7 sts in p, work across rem 5 sts. Place these rem sts on a holder.

With the RSF, attach yarn and work pat as established across the center 26 sts, casting on 1 st at beg and end of row—28 sts. Work 11 rows even. Bind off 7 sts at beg and end of next row. Place center 14 sts on holder. Break yarn. Attach yarn; finish Left Front to correspond to Right Front.

Hand-sew the shoulder and underarm seams.

HOOD: With the RSF, k across all sts from holders—24 sts. Work even for 3 inches. Bind off. Fold hood in half and sew top seam.

SLEEVES (make two): With small straight needles and green yarn, cast on 20 sts. Work Border as for coat. Change to larger needles and st st to work Chart 2, *left, bottom. Note:* Work each edge st with red. Work 25 rows even. Bind off. Set sleeves into coat.

BORDER: Use green yarn and begin at the right front bottom corner. With RSF, crochet a sl st in the running thread bet the edge st and the next st. Continue to crochet sl sts in this way, at a rate of 3 sl sts to 4 knitted rows.

Turn, with smaller dpns and green yarn, pick up and k a st in the top edge of each sl st. Change to ecru and k 2 rows; k 1 row green; bind off knitwise with green.

Making Santa's bag
With the larger dpns and black, cast on 32 sts. Arrange on 3 dpns and join to work in rnds. Beg at base, k 1 rnd.

Inc rnd 1: K 7, **pick up horizontal strand of yarn lying between st just worked and next st and knit into the back of it (m-1 made),** k 2, m-1, k 14, m-1, k 2, m-1, k 7. K 36 sts.

Inc rnd 2: K 8, m-1, k 2, m-1, k 16, m-1, k 2, m-1, k 8—40 sts. K every rnd for 2½ inches. Follow Chart 1, *left, top.* With black k 2 rnds, p 1 rnd, bind off knitwise.

CORD FOR BAG: Cut four 48-inch-long strands of red yarn. Tie one end of each strand around a doorknob. Twist the strands into a rope about 14 inches long; knot the ends. Sew knots to sides of bag.

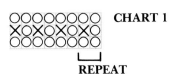

CHART 1

⌐ ⌐
REPEAT

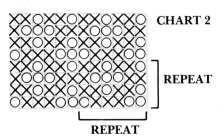

CHART 2

REPEAT

REPEAT

COLOR KEY
⊠ RED
⊘ WHITE

Acknowledgments

We express our gratitude and appreciation to the many people who helped the editors in creating this book.

Our heartfelt thanks to the following designers who contributed material that was especially designed for this book, to the photographers, for their creative contributions, to the companies who generously shared their products with us, and to all those who in some other way contributed to the production of this book.

Design Credits

Rene Anderson—78
Bette Ashley—18, 68
Nadine Bozek—130
Heidi Boyd—106–109
Diane Brakefield—30
Polly Carbonari—16, 121
Cross Stitch & Country
   Crafts—62, 134–135
Susan Douglas—158
Phyllis Dunstan—59, 80, 102–103,
   127, 133, 139, 140, 147, 154
Pam Dyer—14, 153
Stacy Edwards—73, 152
Linda Emmerson—40
Katherine Eng—76–77
Kathy Engel—12
Dixie Falls—65
Joanne Foley—131
Barb Forbes—13
Linda Gillum for Kooler
   Design Studio—74
Jan Hollebrands—37–39
Cindy Hurlbut—116, 122, 136
Jean Kievlan for Suzanne McNeill
   Design Originals—8, 9 (top)
Jan Kornfiend—142
Karen Logsdon—10, 128
Sally Mavor—54–55
Della May—9, birdhouse
Judy McClure—71
Eitha Myhand—49
Nancy Reames—29
Margaret Sindelar—15
Suzie Treinen—34–35, 110–114
Dee Wittmack—28, 36, 104–105

Photo Credits

Hopkins Associates—26–27, 29, 30,
   35, 36, 39, 48–49, 65, 78, 154, 158

Scott Little—47, 61, 62, 68, 73, 76,
   81, 101, 115, 116, 122, 133–136,
   140–153

Perry Struse—6–25; 28, 34–35,
   36–37, 38–39, 40–43, 54–55, 59,
   71, 74–75, 77, 80, 82–100,
   102–114, 120–121, 127–131, 139

If you would like to order any additional copies of our books, call 1-800-678-2802 or check with your local bookstore.

Other Contributors

Evelyn Anderson

Brunswick Yarns
P.O. Box 276
Pickens, SC 29671

Kim Downing

Paul Ecke Poinsettia Ranch
P.O. Box 488
Encinatas, CA 92024

Fabric Traditions®
1350 Broadway
New York, NY 10018
   fabrics for cover, dividers
   All That Glitters #1035 © 1990

The Gifted Line
999 Canal Boulevard
Point Richmond, CA 94804

Groomingdale's
801 73rd Street
Des Moines, IA 50312
   dog bed, page 99

Hallmark Cards, Inc.
Kansas City, MO 64141

C. M. Offray & Son, Inc.
261 Madison Avenue
New York, NY 10016
   wire-edged ribbon, pages 34–35

Peking Handicrafts
1365 Lowrie Avenue
South San Francisco, CA 94080
   crocheted doilies, page 29

Mr. and Mrs. Gene Hosier

Mr. and Mrs. Mark Pennington

Martin Schmidt & Sons
262 NW Miller Road
Portland, OR 97229

The Shoe Store
603 Franklin
Pella, IA 50219
   wooden shoes, page 100